EASY SINGER STYLE™

quick and easy
sewing with your serger

15 easy-sew projects that build skills, too

becky hanson

Creative Publishing
international

contents

5   Welcome to Serging!

about the serger

8   How Sergers Stitch

9   Serger Styles

9   Serger Parts

12   Presser Feet

13   Accessories

sewing with a serger

18   Threading and Thread Tension

18   Setting the Stitch Size

19   Getting the Hang of It

serger stitches

24   3-Thread Overlock Stitch

24   4-Thread Overlock Stitch

24   5-Thread Safety Stitch

25   2-Thread Chain Stitch

25   Cover Stitch

26   Flatlock Stitch

26   2-Thread Overedge Stitch

26   Rolled Hem Stitch

threads, tools, and notions

30	All-Purpose and Serger Threads
30	Specialty Threads
31	Measuring Tools
31	About Fabric Grain
32	Marking Tools
32	Cutting Tools
33	Seam Ripper, Pins, and Pincushions

remaking clothing

37	*Project: Tunic Transformation*
38	Sewing Cover Stitch
41	*Project: Embellished Skirt*
43	Threads for the Overedge Stitch
45	*Project: T-Shirt Shrug*
48	About Ribbing
51	*Project: Faux Vintage Sweater*
52	Getting Ready to Gather

home décor

59	*Project: Cozy Blanket with Overlock Binding*
63	*Project: Reversible Cover-Stitch Pillow*
67	*Project: Wire-Edged Ribbon Bow*
69	Tying the Bow
69	More Bows!
71	*Project: Ribbon-trimmed Table Runner*
75	*Project: Simple Curtains*
77	Blind Hemming
79	*Project: Curtain Tiebacks*
81	Prepping for Piping

fashions and accessories

85	*Project: Thread-Chain Tassel*
87	More Tassels!
89	*Project: Fringed Wrap*
91	Flatlock Stitching on a Fold
95	*Project: Rolled Rosettes*
97	More Rosettes!
99	*Project: Hip Belt*
100	Decorative Chain Stitching
102	Attaching Cord with a Beading Foot
105	*Project: Tiered Skirt*
107	One-Step Gather-and-Sew

111	Suppliers
112	Index

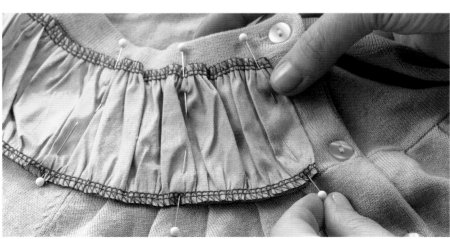

welcome to serging!

Have you ever wondered how store-bought garments or home décor items get those perfectly stitched finished seams? Well, you can achieve this same professional finish on your own projects—with the help of a serger!

A serger, also known as an overlock machine, is different from a standard sewing machine. Although both machines sew stitches, they sew them differently. Each machine works best for different aspects of the sewing process. Just as a kitchen has a stove and a microwave oven, every sewing room should have a sewing machine and a serger. A serger makes many of your sewing tasks faster and easier. It also allows you to create many specialty effects that aren't possible with your sewing machine.

Once you start working with a serger, you'll be amazed at how much time you'll save. You'll love the results, too. Soon, you'll wonder how you ever got along without one!

Have fun! You can sew it!

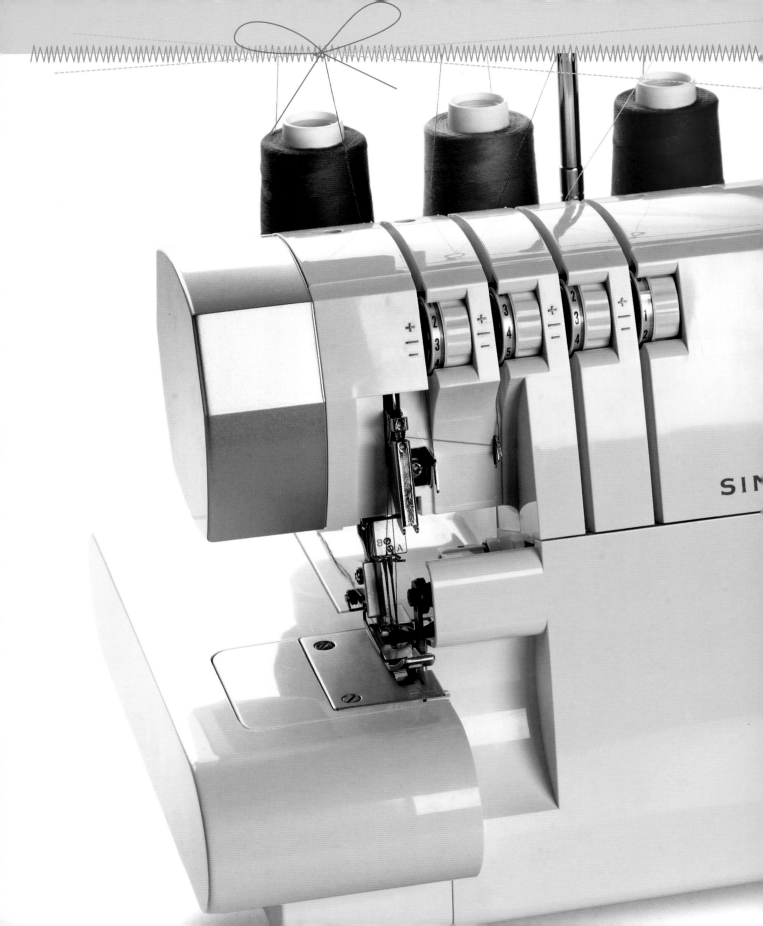

about
the serger

If you have never sewn with a serger, you are in for a treat! Sergers are wonderful machines that trim the fabric edge, overcast it, and sew a seam all at the same time. They also sew lovely embellishment stitches and quick, tightly rolled hems. Your serger will soon become one of the most useful tools in your sewing room. It's not difficult to use—and you'll soon appreciate how much more quickly you can sew and how professional looking your finished results will be!

How Sergers Stitch

How is a serger different from a standard sewing machine? One of the biggest differences is how the stitches are formed. A standard sewing machine has two threads: an upper thread, which goes through the needle, and a bobbin thread. When you sew, the threads meet within the fabric, locking together to form a stitch. A serger doesn't have a bobbin. Instead, it has loopers, which are curved, moving arms with an eye in one end. The looper carries thread fed from a spool through a series of guides. Your machine may have two or three loopers, depending on the type of serger it is.

The loopers work with the needle (or needles, depending on your serger and the type of stitch you are making). Together, they "knit" the stitch onto the fabric's edge. Loopers do not pierce the fabric. Instead, they lay stitches on the top and bottom surfaces of the fabric and "lock" them along the fabric's edge, catching the thread from the moving needle. Sergers are also sometimes called overlock machines.

As the fabric approaches the presser foot on a serger, it passes under a moving knife blade, which trims away any excess fabric. The blade cuts the seam allowance to the exact width of the stitches that wrap the edge. Because the serger trims, stitches, and finishes the edge all at the same time, you can quickly and easily sew perfect, finished seams in one pass.

With your serger, you can make seams to join two pieces of fabric, finish edges, gather ruffles, and sew on trims. But this wonderful machine does much more than utilitarian work—it can sew many decorative effects and finishes, especially if you use special, novelty threads that add dimension or sheen. See Serger Stitches on page 23.

For some tasks, you'll still need your sewing machine—for example, for basting a seam, topstitching, or creating buttonholes. But as you'll learn as you make the projects in this book, the serger and sewing machine are perfect complements. Together they can help you stitch just about anything! You'll soon discover ways of combining the best of both machines to get fast, professional results.

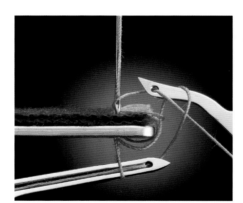

A serger forms stitches by interlocking the threads in the needle and loopers. The loopers do not pierce the fabric. Instead, they lay thread over the fabric surfaces. The needle and loopers work together to lock threads along the fabric edge.

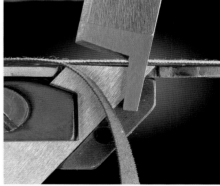

As you sew, the serger's knife blades trim the excess seam allowance before the fabric reaches the needle and loopers.

Serger Styles

There are several different types of sergers. They are categorized by the number of threads they can use. The more threads a serger can use, the more complex its stitches can be—and the more versatile it is. Most sergers available today are either 4-thread or 5-thread machines. Both types sew a strong seam and a variety of stitches. If you come across a 3-thread serger, it's probably an older model, which is still great for finishing edges but doesn't sew as strong a seam.

Most 4-thread sergers can sew with 2, 3, or 4 threads. A 5-thread serger can sew with 2, 3, 4, or 5 threads. With different brands and models, however, there is some variation as to the stitches and functions available. Refer to your machine manual to learn about the stitch capabilities of your specific model, or if you are shopping for a serger, be sure to ask the sewing machine retailer to explain what each model can and cannot do.

Serger Parts

Some serger parts are similar to the parts of a standard sewing machine, but other parts are unique to sergers. Models also differ from each other, so consider your machine manual your best friend as you're getting started. Once you learn the basics of your machine, you'll have all the confidence you need to serge creatively!

Needles

Serger needles vary in style and size, just as they do for a standard sewing machine. Some models work with a universal needle, which may either have a flat or a round shank. Check your owner's manual and always work with the type required for your machine—the styles are not interchangeable. Your machine may accommodate two or three needles, although you won't use them all for every stitch. Your manual will explain how many needles you need for the stitch and where to position them.

Just as when sewing with a sewing machine, you should match the size and style of the serger needle to the type of fabric you are stitching. The wrong needle can damage your fabric or prevent the stitches from forming properly. Industrial-style needles are designed to work with all types of fabric. Most fabrics can be sewn with the universal needle, however, which, as its name implies, is designed to work with many types of fibers and weave structures. Some knits may require a ballpoint needle, which is specially shaped to pierce the fabric without damaging it. Some tightly woven fabrics may require a sharp needle. Keep a variety of needles on hand. To get the best results, always test the needle by stitching on a scrap of your fabric before starting your project.

There is no set rule as to how often you need to change the needle in a serger, but a dull or damaged needle may produce irregular stitches or even cause the thread to break. You can often easily fix these problems just by changing the needle.

Serger needles are available in types and sizes to suit all kinds and weights of fabric.

Loopers

Sergers have an upper looper and a lower looper. These two loopers move back and forth, over or under the fabric, but not through it. The loopers guide the thread, which interlocks with the needle threads to form stitches. Five-thread sergers have an additional looper, called a chain-stitch looper, which allows you to sew an even greater variety of stitches.

Loopers have a much larger eye than does the machine needle, and can accommodate many types of decorative thread that are too thick to pass through the eye of the needle. You can place decorative threads in one or both loopers, depending on the stitch you've selected and the way you want it to look.

Tension Dials

No matter how many threads there are, each one travels through its own tension disk and has its own tension adjustment dial or lever. Sergers are very responsive to thread tension, and small variations in the tension can really change the way a stitch forms and appears. When you thread your machine, always check that the thread is properly engaged in the tension dials and in all the thread guides.

You rarely need to change the tension on a standard sewing machine. On a serger, however, you may often adjust the tension to get the effect you want for different kinds of threads or stitches. Some machines even have an automatic tension device that makes the correct adjustments for you!

In general, the lower the tension settings, the looser the thread tension and the more thread goes into the stitch. Higher settings produce tighter thread tension and allow less thread into the stitch. By adjusting the tension, you can fine-tune the stitch formation. To see how the tension-dial settings affect a particular stitch, thread your serger with a different color thread in each of the needles and loopers. Stitch a small sample as you increase or decrease the tension in small increments. Experiment with one tension dial at a time. This process will help you better understand how the stitches are formed, too.

Blades

Sergers have both an upper blade and a lower blade. When the machine is sewing, the upper blade moves up and down, next to the lower stationary blade, cutting the fabric in its path—just like a mini pair of scissors.

Although it's often handy to have the fabric trimmed away, there are times when you don't want this to happen. For example, if you are embellishing a project and want the embellishment to run across the middle of your fabric, or at some distance from the edge, you certainly don't want

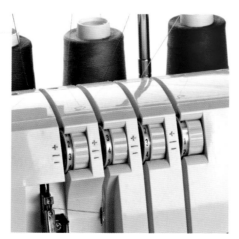

Sergers have two loopers, which carry thread back and forth, over or under the fabric, but not through it.

Dials control the thread tension, which can be made tighter or looser to change the appearance of the stitches.

A pair of sharp blades trims excess fabric before it reaches the needle, leaving an allowance the exact size of the serger stitch.

the fabric chopped off as you stitch! To keep the serger from trimming fabric, simply disengage the upper blade. Depending on the machine, you may adjust a knob or lever to move the upper blade. (The project directions in this book will alert you to disengage the blade when necessary.)

If you notice that the fabric edge is not as neatly trimmed as you'd like, it's probably time to replace the lower blade. Replace the upper blade when you see a nick or other signs of damage on it. The upper blade, usually made of carbide steel, may last from one to five years. Refer to your manual to see what kind of blades to use and how to change them. Discard old blades and buy new ones—don't try to reuse them. Never sew over pins; it will damage the blades and destroy your pins.

Stitch Finger

The stitch finger is a metal prong (or prongs) on the needle plate of the machine. As you sew, the loopers place the threads around the stitch finger and the fabric edge at the same time. The finger supports the fabric so it doesn't collapse inside the moving threads. As the fabric moves through the machine, the stitched edge is fed off the back of the finger.

You may need a narrower stitch finger for some tasks, such as making a rolled hem. On some machines, you can make the stitch finger narrower by simply pushing a lever. On others, you may need to change the needle plate. Check your owner's manual for specific directions for your machine.

Differential Feed

If you look under the presser foot, you will see the feed dogs—the rows of projecting metal teeth that pull the fabric under the presser foot as you sew. The feed dogs make the fabric pass under the foot evenly, whether you are sewing fast or slowly. Many sergers have a differential feed, which means they have two sets of feed dogs: The front set pushes the fabric under the presser foot while the back set pulls the fabric away from it.

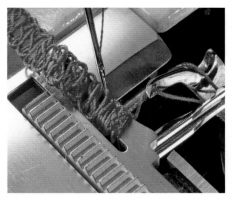

The stitch finger supports the stitches while they are being formed.

On the normal setting, the front and back feed dogs move at the same rate of speed, so that the fabric is fed through the machine evenly. But you can also set them to move at different speeds.

When you increase the speed of the differential feed, the fabric moves toward the presser foot faster than it moves out behind it. It is gathered as

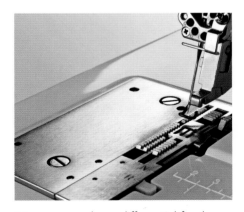

Many sergers have differential feed—two sets of feed dogs that can be set to move at different speeds. They make it easy to create special effects, such as ruffles.

it is sewn, with the fullness secured by the stitches. This setting will help keep stretchy fabrics from becoming "wavy" when stitched. If you decrease the speed of the differential feed, the fabric is stretched as it passes under the foot. This setting helps prevent slippery or lightweight fabrics from puckering.

Your manual will explain how to adjust the differential feed on your serger and probably provide more information on how and why to use this feature for different sewing tasks. (The project instructions in this book indicate how to set the differential feed, if an adjustment is necessary.)

Presser Feet

Depending on your machine type, you can choose from a variety of presser feet. Every serger comes with at least one—this is a standard foot designed for sewing seams and finishing edges. There are many specialty feet available, too. These not only help make some sewing processes easier—such as making blind hems or inserting elastic—but they also expand the creative stitching possibilities on your machine. Whether you want to do decorative serging, home décor, or garment construction, these specialized feet will expand your serger's versatility and your creative options!

Presser feet are designed to fit specific brands and, sometimes, specific models of sergers. Although they may perform the same function, presser feet are not necessarily interchangeable from model to model. Check your manual or ask your sewing machine retailer to learn which feet are available for your serger and how to use them. Here are some types of feet you'll find useful for making the projects in this book.

Shirring Foot

With a shirring foot, you can gather a piece of fabric as you sew it to a second piece, which remains flat. This technique makes it easy to add a ruffle to almost any project. It's quick, and the results are impressive.

Cording Foot

The cording foot makes it possible to sew piping to a project. Piping is a ready-made decorator cord attached to cloth tape, although you can make your own piping, too. The foot has a groove on the bottom that sits on top of the piping and guides the bulky cord past the needle as you stitch.

Beading Foot

The beading foot has a groove on the top. This foot allows you to attach strings of pearls, cord, beads, or other trims to your fabric. The size of the groove determines how wide the trim

Shirring foot

Cording foot

Beading foot

can be. Try the foot with a 2- or 3-thread flatlock stitch (page 26), choosing the left or right needle position (the needle position depends on the thickness of the trim).

If you don't want the thread to show, work with transparent monofilament thread in the needle and the loopers. Fold the fabric to create an edge where you want to attach the trim. Be sure to disengage the blades if you do not wish to trim away any of the fabric (for example, if you are adding trim as a border along an edge).

Yarn Application Foot

The yarn application foot, also known as the gimp foot, has a small slot in the front, which guides yarns, cords, or specialty threads past the needle, allowing you to create a variety of edge finishes. This foot is especially useful for guiding wire or fishing line

into a rolled hem—both of which give the hem edge more body.

Blind-Hem Foot

To make a blind hem, you fold the fabric in such a way that the needle barely pierces it and the thread is nearly invisible from the right side (see page 77). The blind-hem foot guides the folded fabric under the foot, keeping it correctly aligned with the needle.

Taping Foot

This foot is designed for inserting a fabric tape, such as twill tape or tricot bias tape, into garment seams for added stability. It's also great for creating your own trims by serging with decorative thread onto a fabric tape, as for the Embellished Skirt project on page 41. Experiment to see if you want to disengage the upper blade or leave it active so it trims away the extra cloth tape as you stitch.

Accessories

Most sergers come with an assortment of accessories, and the options vary depending on the model. Check your manual to learn about the accessories for your particular machine and how to work with them correctly. You can purchase additional machine accessories and notions from your sewing machine retailer. Here are some of the basic accessories you'll want to have.

Tweezers

Tweezers are a must-have accessory for serging. The long handles and fine tips make them indispensable for threading needles and loopers. Clasp the end of the thread between the tips of the tweezers and guide it into the eye of the looper or needle. If you don't have a special needle-inserting tool, tweezers are also helpful when removing and inserting needles. Sewing machine retailers often carry

Yarn application foot

Blind-hem foot

Taping foot

an assortment of tweezers in various sizes. There are also different types of special looper threaders available—but tweezers work just fine.

Thread Nets

Certain threads, such as rayon sewing thread, Pearl Crown Rayon, metallic thread, rayon floss, and others, create beautiful finished effects. They are often quite slippery, however, which may make them challenging to work with. Thread nets prevent specialty threads from slipping off their spools and tangling. Just slip the net over the spool before placing it on the thread stand. If the net extends beyond the top of the spool, turn it down (like a turtleneck collar).

Spool Caps

Most spools of serger thread are cone-shaped, but you can also work with standard cylindrical spools. If you are working with standard spools, place spool caps (sometimes called unreeling disks) on top of them to help the thread feed evenly through the serger thread path. The caps also keep the thread from catching on any of the spool's rough edges and help to hold the spool on the thread stand.

Cone Adapter

The thread stand of a serger is fitted with spool pins that hold standard cylindrical spools of thread. These pins don't provide the stability needed for the wide, open base of thread cones. Cone adapters are plastic gadgets that slide onto the pins to provide a snug fit for the cones. They usually come with the serger, but you can buy them separately if they are not included or if you misplace one.

Looper Threaders

These long, flexible wire devices are useful for threading the eye of a hard-to-reach looper or needle.

Thread nets keep thread from slipping off the cone and tangling.

Spool caps keep thread on regular spools—versus the cone spools most sergers use—feeding evenly through the thread path.

To stabilize a thread cone on the thread stand, insert a cone adapter before placing the cone on the stand.

Large-Eye Hand-Sewing Needle

Serger stitching leaves a thread tail or thread chain hanging at corners or at the ends of seams. To secure these threads and strengthen the seam ends, you'll need a large tapestry needle or a yarn needle. If the thread ends are on the right side of the fabric, pull them to the wrong side. Insert the thread ends or chain into the eye of the needle and gently slide the needle and thread under the stitches on the wrong side of the project, as shown in the photo below. Bring it out after an inch or so and cut off the excess thread tail.

Work with a hand-sewing needle with a large eye to weave thread tails under a serged seam.

Brush

As you sew, the serger blades cut the fabric, producing a great amount of lint. The lint accumulates in the blade area, under the needle plate, and in the looper area inside the front cover. Frequently sweep away the fiber dust and lint with a small, inexpensive bristle brush.

Liquid Seam Sealant

To seal serged seam ends and keep the stitches from unraveling, simply dot them with a small drop of this clear liquid. Before the sealant dries, sandwich the area with a pressing mat or a piece of muslin and iron it. The heat will dry the sealant and keep the area soft and supple. Most sealants—there are several brands—are washable and dry-cleanable.

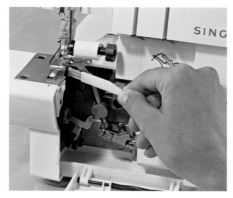

To keep your serger running at its best, frequently brush away the lint that accumulates in the looper area.

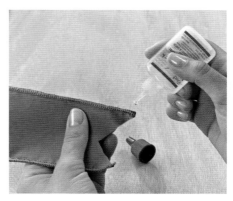

Liquid seam sealant will keep the cut end of serger stitches from unraveling.

sewing with a serger

Before you start your project, take some time to learn how your serger sews. Even if you are familiar with a standard sewing machine, it's a good idea to practice sewing with a serger to get the feel for it. A serger's threading and thread tension are different from a sewing machine's. Also, the serger's blade cuts away part of the seam allowance as you stitch. You should know what to expect and how to guide the fabric through the machine. Once you're comfortable with how the machine works, you'll be ready to dive right in and start sewing!

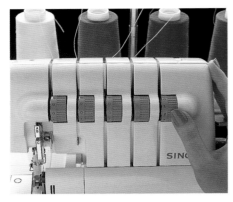

Make sure each thread passes through the tension dial and every guide in its path.

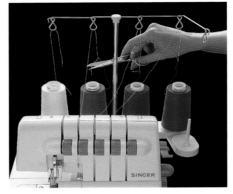

To change thread, you can simply tie the new thread to the old one.

Threading and Thread Tension

In order for the serger to form a perfect stitch and run smoothly, you need to thread it correctly. Incorrect threading can cause broken thread and irregular stitches. It's important to pass each thread through all the guides in its path and to thread the loopers and needles in the order specified in your machine manual. Here are some tips that will help.

Lift the Foot

Be sure to lift the presser foot when threading your serger. When you do, the tension dials open to "receive" the thread. When the presser foot is down, the tension dials are closed and the threads will not really go through them—even though it may appear that the serger is properly threaded.

Tie One On

You don't have to remove the thread from the machine to rethread. You can simply cut the thread close to the spool, change the spool, and tie the new thread to the end of the old one. Tie a square knot and cut the tails so they are about 1" (2.5 cm) long. Lift the presser foot to release the tension dials. Gently pull the thread through the machine (pull only one thread at a time). If the knot is too large to pass through the eye of the needle, clip away the knot and bring the thread through manually.

Check the Tension

The tension settings on your serger are preset at the factory to accommodate standard-weight serger thread. Different threads require different thread tensions. You may also wish to adjust the tension for certain decorative effects. Before you sew a project, always test the stitches to check that the tension is correct. Refer to your manual, and be sure to experiment to see all the options.

Setting the Stitch Size

Serger stitches have both length and width. You can adjust both dimensions to change the way the stitch forms. Sometimes you'll want to make adjustments to accommodate different weights of fabric and types of thread. You'll also make adjustments to create different decorative effects or to apply trims. Your machine manual will explain how to adjust the settings.

Stitch Length

The stitch length is the size of the interval at which the needle pierces the fabric while stitching. If you are sewing a seam, you'll want the stitches to be short so the seam will be strong. If you have decorative thread in the loopers, you may want a longer stitch so the pattern formed by the thread lies smoothly and isn't crowded. If you are making a rolled hem, you may want a very short stitch to create a satin-stitch-like edge.

Stitch Width

On a serger, the stitch width is the distance between the needle thread and the trimmed edge of the fabric. If the stitch width is too narrow, it may not be durable and will not press flat. If the stitch width is too wide, it may cause puckers in the seam.

When you adjust the width setting on a serger, you are really adjusting the position of the blades—and the amount of fabric between the cut edge and the needle. The width of the stitch pattern itself does not change. If your stitches hang off the edge of the fabric, adjust the stitch width so less fabric is trimmed away.

The needle position (left or right) and the thread tension can also affect the stitch width. If the needle is in the left position, the stitch will be wide. If the needle is in the right position, the stitch will be narrow. If the looper tensions are too tight, they could pull in the fabric edge, even causing the fabric to buckle.

Spend time experimenting to see how the stitches change when you adjust the stitch-width setting. Open the looper cover to see how the blade moves when you change it. On some serger models, you adjust the stitch

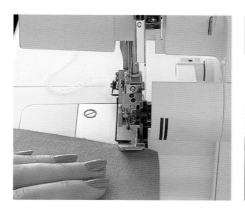

To begin a seam, sew a short chain of stitches before you feed the fabric under the presser foot.

width by changing the needle plate. Check the manual to see how your machine works.

Getting the Hang of It

Even if you have worked with a standard sewing machine, sewing with a serger takes a little practice. It's a good idea to practice guiding the fabric past the blade and needle. Two reasons: First, you can't stitch in reverse, so you need a different way to start and end seams and rows of decorative stitching. Second, the blade makes maneuvering around corners and curves a little bit awkward, and any fabric trimmed away by mistake can't be put back. Following are some tips to get you started.

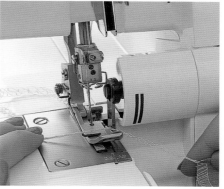

To end the seam, continue sewing past the edge of the fabric until another thread chain forms.

Starting and Ending Seams

When you start sewing with a serger, you rarely put the fabric under the presser foot. All you need to do is to place the fabric up against the front of the presser foot and start sewing! The feed dogs will grab the fabric in front of the presser foot and move it under the foot. The stitches will form a chain that slides off the stitch finger before the fabric reaches the needle. This chain will keep the stitches from pulling apart at the end of the seam or line of decorative stitching.

To begin sewing, bring the thread tails under the presser foot and then to the left of the machine. Gently hold on to the thread tails and begin sewing until you have formed a 3" to 5" (8 to 13 cm) chain. Then place the fabric on the feed dogs in front of the foot.

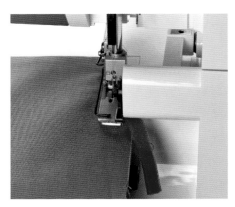

Measure the seam allowance width from the leftmost needle to the cut edge of the fabric—before the fabric reaches the blade.

To end the seam, simply continue sewing past the edge of the fabric until another thread chain forms. Cut the threads, leaving a 3" to 5" (8 to 13 cm) chain attached to the seam and the same amount extending from the serger.

Planning for the Seam Allowance

The serger trims the fabric as it sews. Practice on scrap fabric to become familiar with where the knife blades are, how they work, and how to guide the fabric as you sew the seam. Watch the blade rather than the needles. Cutting mistakes cannot be fixed!

The width of the seam allowance is determined by the position of the leftmost needle. When serging two pieces of fabric, the seam forms where that needle stitches. If the seam allowance is 1/2" (1.3 cm), for example, the edge of the fabric *before it is trimmed* should be 1/2" (1.3 cm) to the right of the leftmost needle. Then, as the fabric moves through the serger, the blade will trim the fabric and the needle will form stitches in position for the correct seam allowance. (The project directions provide the width of the seam allowance you'll need.)

Your machine may already have preset markings on the looper cover to help you position and guide the edge of the fabric. If not, measure with a transparent grid ruler and place a piece of masking tape, marked with various widths, on the looper cover. Remember, if you adjust the stitch width, the cutting blade is in a new position, so you need to work with new guidelines to be sure you are trimming the right amount.

Sewing Curves and Corners

The presser foot on a serger is longer than the presser foot on a standard sewing machine. Because of this extra length, it can be difficult to see where to turn the fabric as you stitch corners and curves. You can't stitch up to the turning point and pivot on an inside corner, as you can on a sewing machine, because the blade in front of the needle will cut the fabric. You can't pivot to sew an outside corner, either. The threads are chained around the stitch finger, so the fabric is "locked" behind the presser foot. Here are some ways to get around these challenges. When sewing curves, watch the knife instead of the needles as you sew. Slightly increase the differential feed (if your machine has this feature) to help ease the fabric and avoid overstretching the fabric edge.

To sew an inside curve, stitch and trim as you would a straight edge, but move the fabric toward the left in front of the presser foot.

To sew an outside curve, guide the fabric by gently moving it to the right in front of the presser foot. If you are sewing a complete circle, overlap the beginning stitches slightly and then stop sewing. Raise the presser foot and shift the fabric so that it is behind the needle. Then stitch straight off the edge.

To sew around an outside corner, sew toward the corner, trimming the fabric as usual. Stop sewing a few inches (centimeters) before you reach the corner. With scissors, trim away about 2" (5 cm) of the seam allowance on the intersecting edge. Sew to the corner and stop when you reach the edge. Then sew one stitch past the edge. Clear the stitch finger (page 11). Pivot the fabric and align the trimmed edge with the blade. Insert the needle

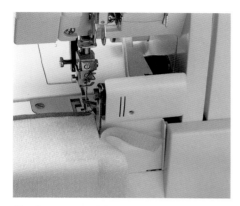

Sewing an outside corner

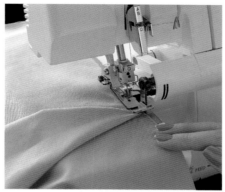

Sewing an inside corner

at the back edge of the fabric. Lower the presser foot and continue. The stitches will overlap at the corner. (Instead of trimming the seam allowance on the intersecting edge, you can also cut the fabric to the finished size with scissors and stitch with the edge aligned with the blade.)

To sew an inside corner, sew toward the corner, stopping when the blade reaches the intersecting edge. Swing the fabric to the left, so the corner becomes a straight edge. Begin to sew again, holding the fabric in a straight line. When the back of the presser foot has cleared the corner, relax the tension on the fabric and sew as usual.

Removing Stitches

Sometimes, you just can't avoid mistakes. We all have had to rip out stitches at one time or another. Luckily, it's easy to remove serged stitches.

To remove overlock stitches, you need to cut one of the looper threads. Carefully slide the blade of a seam ripper between the stitches and fabric. Then pull the remaining threads from the fabric.

To remove a chain stitch, pull the looper thread out of the last loop at the end of the stitches with a straight pin. Then lift this thread to help bring the needle thread through to the other side of the fabric. Gently pull the looper thread to unravel the stitches. Remove the loose needle thread.

Remove cover-stitch threads just as you would remove chainstitch threads. With a seam ripper or a straight pin, remove the last two or three stitches formed by each of the needle threads. Turn over the fabric and gently pull on the looper thread until all the stitches unravel. Remove the loose needle threads.

To remove flatlock stitches, carefully undo them one at a time with a straight pin or simply pull the lower looper thread.

When restitching the area where you've removed stitches, remember that, unless the blade was disengaged, the excess seam allowance has already been trimmed away. Guide the fabric edge along the left side of the blade so that no more fabric is cut off.

serger stitches

There are many wonderful serger stitches. Each stitch is especially suited to a different type of sewing, but you can creatively embellish with them, too—especially if you work with decorative thread.

Which stitches you use, and how you use them, depends in part on the type of serger you have—each type has a different number of threads, needles, and loopers (page 9). After you've chosen a stitch, you may need to thread your serger in a specific way, change the needle position, adjust the tension, change the presser foot, or disengage the blade—so always check the machine manual for the specific setup. Here are some of the basic stitches you'll work with as you make the projects in this book.

3-thread overlock stitch

3-thread overlock stitch as a decorative edging

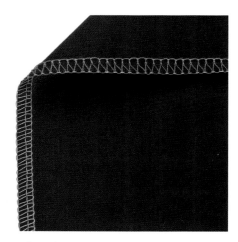

4-thread overlock stitch

3-Thread Overlock Stitch

The 3-thread overlock stitch is the basic serger stitch. It is formed with two loopers and one needle. This stitch is often used to clean-finish seam allowances on seams that are already sewn with a straight stitch on a standard sewing machine. This stitch isn't strong enough to use for sewing together two pieces of fabric.

The 3-thread overlock stitch is a good stitch for sewing a blind hem, which barely shows on the right side of the project, as in the Simple Curtains project on page 75.

With decorative threads in the loopers, you can also create a bold or fancy finish with the 3-thread overlock. If your serger has two needle positions, you can change the width of the stitch by placing the needle on the left to make a wide stitch, or on the right to make a narrow stitch (see Setting the Stitch Size, page 18).

The 4-Thread Overlock Stitch

The 4-thread overlock stitch is made with two needle threads and two looper threads. This stitch looks very much like a wide 3-thread overlock stitch, but it has an additional reinforcement thread. The 4-thread overlock stitch makes a fairly strong seam, so it's the right choice for sewing together two pieces of lightweight or medium-weight fabric. It's also flexible, so it's good for stretch fabrics. This stitch is sometimes called a 4-thread mock-safety stitch.

5-Thread Safety Stitch

You often find the 5-thread safety stitch in ready-to-wear garments. If you look closely, you can see that it is actually a 3-thread overlock stitch with a parallel line of stitching running alongside it. That line of stitching is a 2-thread chain stitch.

None of the projects in this book require the 5-thread safety stitch, but it's good to know how to use it. This stitch does not stretch, so it's best when you need a very stable stitch that can hold up under stress. This stitch is an excellent choice for serging medium-weight to heavyweight woven fabrics, or when sewing seams you don't want to stretch in knit fabrics. If your machine can sew this stitch, you can set it to sew the chain stitch only, without the overlock, as shown on the facing page.

2-Thread Chain Stitch

The 2-thread chain stitch is a feature of the 5-thread safety stitch, but you can also use it by itself—for example, to add decorative work, as in the Hip Belt project on page 99. Some 4-thread sergers also sew a chain stitch. To sew the chain stitch alone, disengage the upper blade of the serger. If the blade isn't cutting the fabric, you can stitch with a wide seam allowance or embellish the interior portion of your project. The chained loops of thread form on the side of the fabric that faces the feed dogs—not on the side you see while you are sewing—so if you wish to mark your design on the fabric, mark the wrong side.

Cover Stitch

A cover stitch is a special hemming stitch that appears as parallel rows of topstitching on the right side of the project. Some 5-thread sergers can be set up to sew a cover stitch. This stitch provides the hem finish you often see on ready-to-wear knits without ribbing (the stretchy, sewn-on bands at the hem, neck, and cuffs). From the right side, this stitch looks like two, or more, parallel rows of topstitching. From the wrong side, it looks like a row of looped threads.

Always disengage the blade before stitching so that you can sew a hem of any depth without cutting off the folded edge. You can make the cover stitch reversible, too. Place decorative thread in the loopers and sew with the right side of your project down, against the feed dogs, to create a row of cover-stitch embellishment.

2-needle cover stitch sewn with needles in the left- and right-hand positions

5-thread safety stitch

2-needle cover stitch sewn with needles in the left and center positions

2-thread chain stitch

3-needle cover stitch

Some machines sew a 2-thread cover stitch; some sew both 2- and 3-thread cover stitch. If your machine can sew a cover stitch with three needles, you can adjust the width of the 2-thread cover stitch. Use two needles and put them in the left and right positions (for a wide stitch) or in the center and either the right or left position for a narrow stitch.

Flatlock Stitch

The flatlock stitch is a variation of the 3-thread overlock stitch, but it has a completely different look. To make this stitch, you loosen the needle-thread tension and tighten the lower-looper tension. These adjustments create a ladderlike stitch pattern on the side of the fabric that faces the feed dogs.

Use flatlock stitch to make a seam—joining two pieces of fabric—or to sew along a fold. After stitching, you gently open the fabric layers. The seam will lie completely flat, with the cut edges overlapping inside the stitches, and there will be no seam allowance extending on the inside of the project. If the fabric pieces are wrong sides together as you sew, the ladder pattern will be on the wrong side of your project. If the fabric pieces are sewn with the right sides

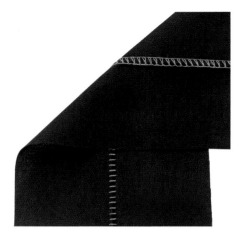

Narrow 3-thread flatlock stitch sewn in the middle of the fabric

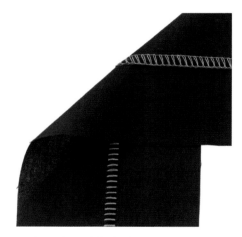

Wide 3-thread flatlock stitch sewn in the middle of the fabric

together, the ladder pattern will be on the right side of your project.

This stitch is a good choice for decorative embellishment—either with a special thread in the looper to create a bold band of stitches, as for the Fringed Wrap on page 89, or with ribbon woven through the ladder "rungs," as for the Ribbon-trimmed Table Runner on page 71.

2-Thread Overedge Stitch

This stitch is a variation of the flatlock stitch. The 2-thread overedge stitch makes a delicate edge finish that is especially nice for lightweight fabric. You thread only the needle and lower looper. The threads "lock" at the fabric edge instead of at the needle.

To make an embellished ribbon, sew this stitch on twill tape, tricot, bias tape, or another type of narrow ribbon. The decorative trim will dress up a simple garment (page 41) or home accessory. Choose an interesting thread for the looper to give the embellished ribbon added dimension. If your serger does not sew a 2-thread overedge stitch, make a 3-thread overedge stitch instead.

Rolled Hem Stitch

A rolled hem stitch is a very fine binding stitch that folds under a narrow margin of fabric as it's sewn. You often find this hem finish on napkins, scarves, and ruffles. The stitch finger (page 11) should be set very, very narrow to cause the fabric to roll under as you sew. Different sergers create this finish in different ways, so check your manual for the correct settings. You might need a rolled hem foot or a special needle plate to sew this stitch.

Depending on your serger, you may be able to sew a rolled hem with two threads or three threads—or have both options (check your manual). A 2-thread version is nice on lightweight fabric. Always test the stitch on scrap fabric cut on the same grain as the edge you'll hem for your project. The tension requirements may be different if the fabric edge is on lengthwise grain, crosswise grain, or bias (page 31).

You can set this stitch to create an open thread pattern or a very tight, satinlike pattern that resembles a trim, depending on your fabric, thread choice, and the project. You can work with decorative thread and add wire or fishing line to stiffen the edge. Because there are so many options, be sure to test and experiment until you get the look you want before you begin your project.

2-thread overedge stitch

2-thread narrow rolled hem

3-thread rolled hem

here's a hint!

Keep a record of your stitching samples so you can re-create them! Write the stitch name, thread name, tension setting, and stitch length and width on a file card or in a notebook. Staple the sample swatch to it.

You can make pretty trim by sewing a 2-thread overedge stitch with decorative thread on twill tape or ribbon.

threads, tools, and notions

There are so many thread choices for serging! You'll work with regular sewing thread to construct your project, but when it's time to add embellishment, you'll enter the world of decorative specialty threads, fine ribbons, and yarns. Threads come in a variety of beautiful fibers. The projects in this book show you how to make the most of these materials.

There are lots of different sewing tools and gadgets, too, but you need only a few basic ones to be all set to sew.

All-Purpose and Serger Threads

Always work with high-quality thread that is strong and won't easily break. Threads should be soft, smooth, evenly spun, and flexible, and should slide easily through thread guides and loopers. Avoid stiff threads and those with a bumpy texture. Choose an appropriate weight for your project fabric and make sure it can be laundered in the same way as the finished piece.

For construction seams, you should work with regular (all-purpose) sewing thread or with serger thread, which is lighter in weight. A serged seam contains a lot more thread than a straight-stitch seam sewn on a standard sewing machine, so the thread doesn't need to be as heavy. Lightweight serger threads make it less bulky, too. You can work with regular thread on small spools, cardboard cylinders, or cones.

Specialty Threads

You'll find specialty threads on spools and cones of various shapes. You'll also find some wound on cards, balls, or skeins, which you'll need to rewind by hand onto an empty spool.

Monofilament thread, heavyweight cotton, topstitching, and textured

Cones hold many yards (meters) of thread.

nylon threads are the easiest to work with on the serger. They require minor tension adjustments and fit through the needles and both loopers.

Monofilament

Monofilament nylon thread is essentially colorless, so it will blend with the color of the fabric—especially effective as the needle thread when making a blind hem or when stitching a rolled hem on multicolored fabric.

Topstitching Thread

Heavyweight cotton and topstitching threads are great for chain stitching, cover stitching, and flatlocking. With these heavy threads, the stitching is more pronounced and adds texture to the fabric. You may need a large size needle for them.

Texturized Nylon Thread

This type of thread, such as Woolly Nylon, comes in both regular and heavy weights. It is versatile and easy to use. When pulled taut, it looks like a regular thread, but when it is relaxed it appears fluffy and covers the fabric surface well. It is sensitive to high heat, so set your iron and dryer to low!

Ribbons

As long as it is soft and pliable, you can place very narrow (2 mm [¹⁄₁₆"]) ribbon, such as silk ribbon, in the serger's loopers. Ribbon Floss, which looks braided, is one good option. You'll find many other types in yarn shops, usually wrapped on a card or in a ball. Avoid polyester ribbon, which is stiff.

Pearl Cotton

Pearl cotton is a twisted thread used for hand embroidery. Size 8 is a suitable size for serging. It comes in small balls or skeins. Pearl Crown is a shiny rayon pearl thread that comes on machine-ready spools.

Metallic Threads

Metallic threads may fray, but they add glitz to your projects. It's worth taking the time to experiment with them! They're fun to shop for, too.

Yarn

If you'd like to try to work with knitting or crochet yarn, go ahead! Look for thin, smooth, tightly twisted yarns that will fit through the thread guides and loopers. Yarn tends to stretch so you may have to loosen the tension quite a bit before you sew it.

Measuring Tools

Sewing requires accurate measuring and cutting. A flexible tape measure is essential for taking body measurements and checking dimensions as you sew. Look for a fiberglass or plastic tape measure at least 60" (153 cm) long. Most are marked in both inches and centimeters. A long metal ruler is best for measuring large dimensions on fabric.

As a guide for marking your cutting and stitching lines, you'll need a transparent acrylic ruler. Choose one with a grid in inches or centimeters or the type designed for quilters, which is rigid and sometimes has both angled and parallel guidelines—a must-have if you are working with a rotary cutter. Another handy tool is a seam gauge, which is a 6" (15 cm) metal ruler with a sliding marker in the center. Use it to quickly check seam and hem allowances.

From the top: a seam allowance ruler, hem gauge, retractable pocket-size tape measure, standard flexible tape measure, and transparent ruler

About Fabric Grain

Fabric is woven from two perpendicular sets of threads, which form a lengthwise straight grain and a crosswise straight grain. The lengthwise threads parallel the selvage (finished edge) of the fabric. The 45-degree angle between the lengthwise and crosswise grains is called the bias (see the drawing at right).

The straight lengthwise and crosswise grains are stable, which means they don't stretch. The bias stretches when pulled by the sewer and by the force of gravity. Knit fabric is formed with one continuous thread secured in a series of interlocking loops. Look at the fabric closely to see how these loops, like woven threads, align lengthwise and crosswise.

To be sure that projects such as garments and curtains hang as they should, position each of the pieces so the grainline is aligned correctly on the fabric as you mark and cut. In most cases, the vertical edges of the piece fall on the lengthwise straight grain; the horizontal edges fall on the crosswise grain.

The fabric pieces for decorative accents—such as piping, bows, or rolled rosettes—are often cut on the bias. For piping, the stretch of the bias helps the fabric fit smoothly around the cord. Bias-cut fabric enhances the drape of the loops and tails of bows. Bias rosettes roll up and flare more evenly than those cut on the straight grain.

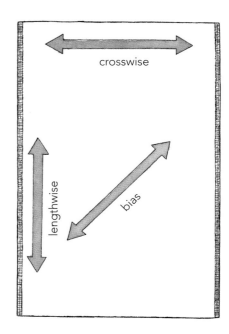

Marking Tools

Marking tools are the pens and pencils of sewing. You'll need them frequently, for every project you make, to mark fabric with temporary cutting lines, seamlines, buttonholes, and other construction details. Most fabric pens, pencils, and chalks make temporary marks that wash out, brush out, or disappear after a few days of exposure to the air. It's always a good idea to test the marker on your fabric to make sure it won't leave permanent marks that will spoil your work.

Easy-to-use chalk dispensing tools leave a precise line that brushes off easily. These tools are great when you are marking fabric just before cutting or sewing. Some chalk markers, especially the wedges known as tailor's chalk, have a waxy ingredient that makes the mark last longer—test

Fabric-marking pencils, an eraser, and a chalk holder and tailor's chalk

From the top: small and large dressmaker's shears, embroidery scissors, and sewing scissors

these first, however, to make sure they don't leave a permanent mark when you iron your fabric.

Cutting Tools

The best cutting tools are easy and comfortable to use. There are several types and sizes, and each is useful in its own way.

Scissors and Shears

Even though we call both of them "scissors," scissors and shears are different tools. Sewing scissors, good for clipping seams and trimming, have two identical handles, each with a round hole for one finger or your thumb. They are about 6" (15 cm) long, with one rounded and one pointed blade. Embroidery scissors are small, with two very sharply pointed blades that are perfect for clipping threads.

The handles on a pair of shears are offset from the blades. One handle has a hole that is large enough for several fingers. The other has a round hole that fits your thumb. The offset blades are designed to glide along the table, so the fabric remains flat as you cut. Shears come in several sizes. Most people find a pair that is 8" or 10" (20 to 25 cm) long most comfortable. You'll also find left-handed shears.

Buy the best scissors and shears you can afford—and don't use them to cut anything but fabric and thread! Paper and cardboard will dull the blades, making them bad for your fabric. Store your cutting tools with your sewing gear so family members don't pick them up for other purposes.

Rotary Cutting Tools

Rotary cutting tools consist of a round revolving blade like a sharp pizza cutter, a self-healing mat to protect the table, and a special rigid ruler. These tools make it possible for you to cut fabric without first marking a cutting line. Both the ruler and mat are marked with a grid of parallel lines so you can align and measure the fabric and accurately guide the cutter. Quilters, who often need many small, same-size geometric pieces, love this cutting system. It's great for other

The cutting mat protects your work surface and provides a measuring guide. The rotary cutter cuts fabric quickly. The transparent ruler measures and also guides the wheel.

types of sewing projects too, if you aren't cutting large or curved shapes.

Rotary cutters come in three sizes: 28 mm, 45 mm (the most convenient), and 60 mm. Be sure to choose one that has a retractable cover to protect the blade and your fingers. Always close the cover when you put the blade down or away. Keep extra blades on hand so you can replace them as they become dull.

Choose a cutting mat that is at least 18" x 24" (45 x 61 cm) so that you can lay a folded width of 45" (114 cm) fabric on it. Clear acrylic rulers come in many shapes and sizes, but a 6" x 24" (15 x 61 cm) size works for most purposes.

Seam Ripper, Pins, and Pincushions

A seam ripper is an essential tool—we all have to rip out stitches at some point! Cut the stitches one at a time, as shown in the top photo below. Or, when removing a band of serger stitches, first slide the long tip of the blade between the stitches and the fabric. Then slowly push the blade

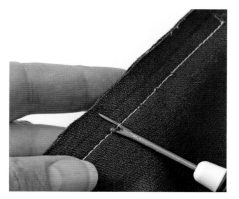

To remove a stitch, insert the long pointed tip of the seam ripper under the stitch and cut the thread with the curved blade.

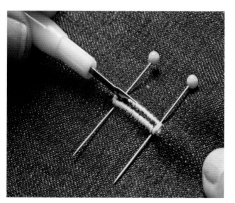

To cut open a buttonhole, first position a pin across each end, inside the stitches, and then insert the tip of the seam ripper and slice the space between the stitches with the curved blade.

against the stitches. You can also cut buttonholes open with a seam ripper.

All-purpose dressmaker pins, which are medium length, are a good size for general sewing. Pins with colored glass heads are easy to see, as are colored plastic-head pins—but be careful with these, as a hot iron can melt them.

Every sewing box needs at least one pincushion. Pincushions come in many shapes and sizes. Choose a classic tomato style (the attached strawberry is filled with resin for sharpening needles and pins!), one that you can wear on your wrist, or a magnetic pincushion that will keep you from having to pick up stray pins—the choice is entirely yours!

Standard or Metric Measurements?

The dimensions in this book have been calculated for easy measurung and sewing in both the standard (also known as English) and metric systems. The equivalents are not consistent because they have been rounded up or down to make the best sense for each part of the process. Follow only one system as you work.

Remaking Clothing

What better place to start shopping for ideas than your own closet! Create brand-new, one-of-a-kind garments from your fashion stash from seasons past or from old Plain Jane clothes that just don't cut it. Quick to finish, these skill-building projects will get you serging like a pro. You'll be diving into your own wardrobe or hunting for chic vintage finds in no time! In this chapter, you'll learn how to make over a simple cardigan sweater with a charming ruffle and turn a so-so T-shirt into a stylish cropped jacket. You'll also learn how to make cover-stitched hems like a Seventh Avenue designer and create fabulous trims that will add fashionable flair to just about anything in your wardrobe!

tunic transformation

With just a few snips and some clever cover-stitch hemming, you can turn a ho-hum crewneck sheath dress into an uptown tunic top. The cover stitch, which is a feature of some 5-thread sergers, creates a hem that looks like two or three parallel lines of topstitching—but with a serger, you can sew them all at the same time!

Machine
- 5-thread serger with 2-needle cover-stitch capability, or a cover-stitch machine

Materials
- long-sleeved knit dress
- three spools of thread to match dress

Notions and Tools
- pins
- scissors
- tailor's chalk
- ruler

Before

tunic transformation

1 Try on the dress and decide where you'd like the new hemlines for the sleeves and body. Mark the position of the hemlines with chalk (you can make just one mark on the body and on one sleeve). Remove the dress and lay it flat.

2 Measure from the chalk mark to the dress's bottom edge. With the chalk, draw a line across the dress at that same distance from the edge. This line is the fold line. With a transparent grid ruler, draw a second line 1" (2.5 cm) below the first. Measure and mark one of the sleeves the same way.

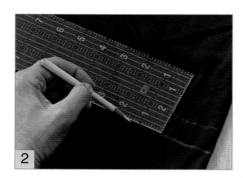

3 Cut the body of the dress along the lower marked line. Cut the sleeve along the lower marked line. Working with the cut-off sleeve as a pattern, cut the same amount off the other sleeve.

4 To mark the stitching line on the body, draw another line 1" (2.5 cm) above the fold line (2" [5 cm] above the cut edge). Fold the bottom of the dress body to the wrong side along the fold line and pin, as shown in the photo. Repeat the process on each sleeve.

5 Set your serger for a wide 2-needle cover stitch, referring to your manual and the sidebar at right. Practice the stitch if you are not familiar with it.

6 Place the dress body in the serger right side up, positioning the stitching line under the left needle. Sew a cover stitch all around the garment, beginning and ending the stitch as explained in the sidebar.

7 Turn the dress inside out. Place the sleeve under the presser foot, as shown in the photo, aligning the stitching line with the left needle. Sew the sleeve hem. Repeat with the other sleeve.

8 Try on the dress again to design the new neckline. On one-half of the dress front, mark a line where you want the neck edge to be. Work with pins if it's hard to draw while looking in the mirror.

9 Remove the dress and lay it flat, with the front side facedown on the table. Fold the entire garment in half lengthwise, turning it so the marked front is faceup. With chalk, redraw the marked or pinned neckline with a bold line. Draw a cutting line parallel to the first line and 1/2" (1.3 cm) closer to the existing neckline of the dress. Pin through all layers to prevent shifting. Cut the dress through all layers along that line.

10 Working all around the newly cut neckline, fold 1/2" (1.3 cm) of fabric to the wrong side, stretching the fabric edge slightly so it lies flat around the curve and pinning it in place. Place the neckline right side up in the serger, positioning the right needle about 1/8" (3 mm) from the folded edge. Stitch the hem to finish.

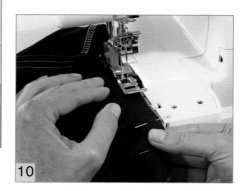

sewing cover stitch

Set the serger for a 2-thread or 3-thread cover stitch, following the instructions in your machine's manual and as specified in the instructions for your project. Be sure to disengage the upper blade and the upper looper.

If you are embellishing with cover stitch, simply test the stitch with the project thread on a single layer of your fabric to make sure the settings are correct. If you'll be sewing a hem, stitch a test hem first. Fold under a hem allowance on a piece of scrap fabric. Place the test hem in the serger, with the hem down, against the feed dogs.

Practice the stitch to keep the needles parallel to the folded edge of the fabric. Adjust the stitch settings and the position of the fabric until your stitches cover the cut edge of the hem on the wrong side of the scrap.

As the serger forms the cover stitch, the needle threads wrap around the looper. You must clear these threads from the looper before you can remove the fabric from the machine.

To do this, instead of sewing off the edge of the fabric as you usually do at the end of a seam, stop stitching at the edge. Raise the needles to the highest position. Then turn the handwheel toward you to bring the needles to their lowest position. Rotate the handwheel backward to return to the starting position. The looper will now be free of the threads, so raise the presser foot and pull the threads away from the machine. Pinch the end of the stitching between your thumb and forefinger as you pull to keep the stitches from coming undone or bunching.

Often, cover stitch is sewn in the round, as when hemming the Tunic Transformation. To end this type of seam, sew over the beginning stitches, overlapping them about 1" (2.5 cm). Then remove the fabric, first clearing the needle threads from the looper. Pull the threads to the wrong side and secure them by tying in a knot or pulling them through the stitching on the inside of the garment with a tapestry or yarn needle (page 15).

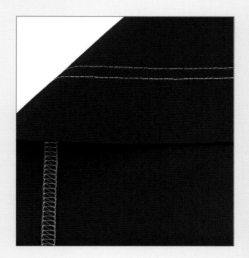

here's a hint!

To make a decorative border on your hem, cover-stitch with the dress wrong side up in the serger.

What a great technique—your new garment looks just like ready-to-wear!

embellished skirt

Here's a great way to make a very fancy trim that will add lots of extra dazzle to your clothes or home accessories. All you need are some decorative threads, a narrow twill tape or ribbon, and the flatlock stitch on your serger. Ribbon Floss is an ideal thread, but the possibilities are endless, so experiment with different decorative threads to find the one you like best.

Before

Machines and Feet
- 3-, 4-, or 5-thread serger with 2-thread overedge stitch capability
- taping foot
- standard sewing machine (with ballpoint needle, if your garment is a knit)

Materials
- A-line skirt (shown here in interlock knit fabric)
- twill tape, 1/2" (1.3 cm) wide, lime or color desired (refer to step 1 to estimate amount)
- Ribbon Floss, gold or color desired (the project shown here required four 5-m spools)
- one spool of sewing thread to match Ribbon Floss

Notions and Tools
- chalk
- pins
- dressmaker's carbon and tracing wheel (optional)
- tape measure
- sewing scissors
- 1/2" (1.3 cm)-wide double-sided fusible basting tape, same amount as twill tape (refer to step 1 for amount)

Note: If your serger does not sew a 2-thread overedge stitch, you may use a 3-thread overedge stitch instead. For this stitch, you will need two spools of sewing thread to match the Ribbon Floss.

embellished skirt

here's a hint!

Arrange string to create your design on the garment. Measure the string to see how much twill tape you'll need. Add more if you change your mind!

1 Lay your garment right side out on your work surface. With chalk or pins, draw the design that you want to embellish with trim. You can copy the design in the photos or create your own. Remember to keep any areas that need to stretch (necklines, cuffs, waistbands) free of trim.

If you want to create a symmetrical design, mark one-half of it on half the garment. Then transfer the mirror image to the other half with dressmaker's carbon and a tracing wheel. Measure the length of the lines to see how much trim you need to make the design.

2 Set your serger for a wide, 2-thread overedge stitch, referring to your machine's manual for specific instructions. If this stitch isn't an option on your machine, set the serger for a 3-thread overedge stitch. Put regular sewing thread in the needle and ribbon floss in the lower looper (page 10). Loosen the tension dial for the decorative thread quite a lot. (If you are using a 3-thread overedge stitch, put the Ribbon Floss in the upper looper and the decorative thread in the needle and lower looper.)

3 Sew a test on a piece of scrap fabric. Adjust the tension so the decorative thread lies flat. If you can't get the tension loose enough, try removing the floss from the tension disk and perhaps from a few thread guides, too.

4 Now test the stitch on the twill tape you're going to work with. Put the taping foot on the serger. Guide the tape into the foot so that the needle is close to the left edge of the tape. As you begin to sew, hold the thread and ribbon floss tails behind the presser foot so they don't tangle in the first stitches.

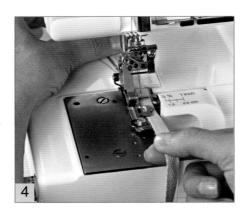

5 Sew some of the twill tape and check the effect. Adjust the settings to create the desired look. When you're happy with the effect, sew the overedge stitch on enough twill tape to make your finished design.

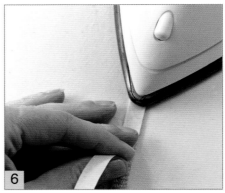

6 Set your iron to the wool setting. Following the package directions, fuse the basting tape to the wrong side of the embellished twill tape.

here's a hint!

To get floss trim to feed smoothly under the presser foot, turn the handwheel manually to make the first few stitches.

7 Lay your garment as flat as possible, right side up. Remove the paper backing from the embellished trim. Arrange the trim on your garment, following your drawn lines, and pin it in place. Fuse the trim onto the garment with the iron. You may remove pins from the flat areas as you go, but it's helpful to leave them in those places where the tape overlaps.

8 Thread a standard sewing machine with thread to match the ribbon floss and set it for a medium-length straight stitch. Sew the trim to the garment, stitching along each edge of the trim.

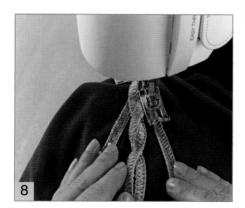

threads for the overedge stitch

Because you are working with only two threads to make the overedge stitch—and each one is a different color—it's easy to see which thread you need to adjust as you fine-tune the stitching. While you're still learning how to make this stitch, stick with acrylic, cotton, rayon, or silk threads, which are all flexible, for the looper. Polyester and nylon tend to be stiff and are more difficult to feed through the machine.

After you've seen how the stitch works, start to experiment. You might choose a metallic ribbon floss to create sparkly elegance, as for this project. Or you might choose a crochet cotton trim for a "boho" look. Solid silk floss will add a quiet and classic touch of contrasting texture and color.

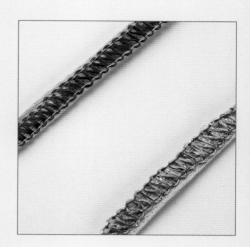

Be dramatic! Intertwine
trim of different colors.

t-shirt shrug

You'll be amazed to see how fun and quick it is to transform an over-sized tee into a fashion statement that has vintage style. Just take that tee and cut it down to size. Then get out your serger and sew on some bands of ribbing with a 4-thead overlock stitch. The end result? A flattering, form-fitting silhouette! Add the finishing touch with oversized buttons for a bit of retro whimsy.

Machine
• 4- or 5-thread serger (to sew 4-thread overlock stitch)

Materials
• approximately $1/2$ yd. (0.5 m) of ribbing fabric
• long-sleeved, oversized T-shirt
• four spools of thread to match T-shirt
• two large snaps (optional)
• two buttons, $1^1/8"$ (2.8 cm) in diameter (optional)

Notions and Tools
• pins
• fabric marker or chalk
• scissors
• transparent grid ruler

Seam Allowance
$1/2"$ (1.3 cm)

Before

t-shirt shrug

1 Try on the shirt to decide where to position the bottom ribbing. The ribbing is $2^{1}/2$" (6.5 cm) deep, so the seamline for the top of the ribbing should be $2^{1}/2$" (6.5 cm) above the desired new hemline. Mark the desired seamline with chalk—you can mark just one place on the body. Mark the seamline on the sleeve in the same way, allowing for 3" (7.5 cm) of ribbing.

2 Remove the shirt and lay it flat. Measure from the chalk mark on the body to the bottom edge. Subtract $^{1}/2$" (1.3 cm) from that measurement. Draw a line all around the shirt at that shorter distance from the bottom edge. Cut the shirt along the line.

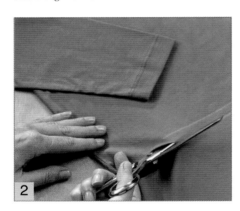

3 Measure, mark, and cut the marked sleeve the same way. Working with the cut-off sleeve as a pattern, cut the same amount off the other sleeve.

4 Lay the shirt flat again, with the front facing up. Measure the width from side seam to side seam. Divide that number in half to find the center front. Chalk-mark the center front in several places along the front of the shirt. With the transparent grid ruler as a guide, draw a line from the bottom to the top of the shirt, connecting the marks.

5 Measuring with the ruler, draw two lines, each $^{1}/2$" (1.5 cm) away from the center front line, as shown in the photo. Cut the shirt along these lines, removing the 1" (3 cm) strip of fabric between them.

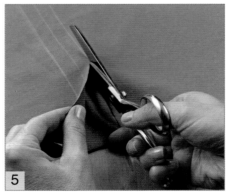

6 Measure and mark a line $1^{1}/2$" (4 cm) below the neck edge. Cut the shirt on this line.

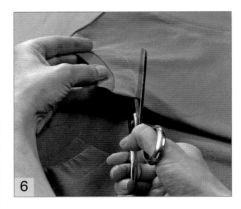

7 Measure around the section of your body where you want the bottom ribbing to sit. Add 2" (5 cm) for the seam allowance and wearing ease. This measurement is the length of ribbing you'll need. Cut a strip of ribbing to that length and 6" (15.5 cm) deep. Make sure the ribs are parallel to the 6" (15.5 cm) edge.

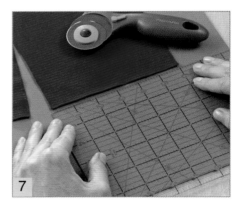

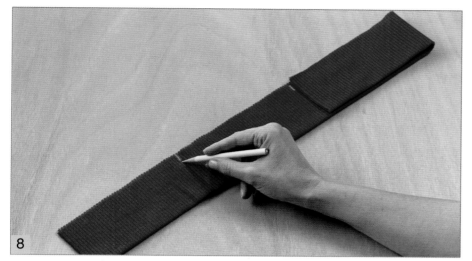

8 Fold the ribbing strip in half lengthwise, right side out. Divide the strip in quarters: Fold it in half crosswise; mark the fold on one raw edge. Unfold the strip. Then fold each end to the mark in the middle, marking each new fold on the same raw edge as the first mark.

9 Along the bottom of the shirt, measure from side seam to side seam to find the center back. Mark the position with chalk or a pin. Lay the shirt right side up on your work surface. Unfold the ribbing and lay it on top of the shirt, with the raw edges aligned, as shown in the photo. Pin the mark in the middle of the ribbing to the mark at the center back of the shirt. Pin one end of the ribbing to each front edge.

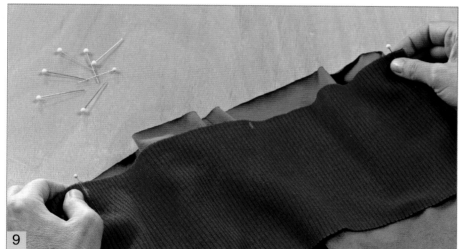

10 Pin each of the other marks on the ribbing to a side seam. Stretch the ribbing to fit the bottom of the shirt and pin the pieces together at 1" (2.5 cm) intervals.

11 Fold the ribbing so the long edges align again and, repositioning one pin at a time, pin it to the shirt through both layers.

12 Set your serger for a standard 4-thread overlock stitch. Place the shirt in the serger with the ribbing on top. Sew the ribbing to the shirt with a 1/2" (1.3 cm) seam allowance (you'll trim off about 1/4" [6 mm]). Remove the pins as you stitch and stretch the ribbing to lie flat against the shirt.

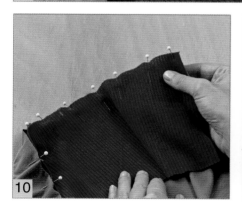

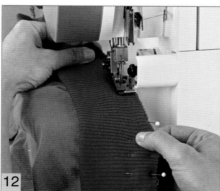

here's a hint!

You can leave the ribbing folded in half when you pin it to the shirt botom, but it may be easier to pin and ease thick ribbing in a single layer.

about ribbing

It's the knit fabric in ribbing that makes these areas of a garment hug your body yet stretch easily over your head, shoulders, hand, or hips when you are dressing. Look closely at the ribbing on your T-shirts, sweatshirts, or knit skirts and pants. You'll see vertical ridges, or ribs, that allow the fabric to stretch and spring back to shape.

Ribbing is almost always made from a strip of fabric that has been folded in half. The two raw edges are sewn to the garment, and the fold forms the edge of the cuff or band.

You can buy ribbed fabric by the yard (meter), just like any other fabric. When cutting strips, be sure to cut along the crosswise grain so the ribs run vertically, which will allow the greatest amount of stretch from side to side. You can sometimes buy ribbing strips that have been precut and folded, sold by the yard (meter) or by the piece.

If you want the ribbing to form a tight band at the edge of your garment—say, for a cuff—the length should be less than the measurement of the garment edge. You'll need to stretch the ribbing to fit the garment edge as you sew them together, but t hen the ribbing will spring back to its snug shape.

You can also add ribbing as a decorative band—for example, a button band along the center front of a garment. In this case, the garment edge and ribbing should be the same length so the ribbing is relaxed as you sew the pieces together.

13 | Measure the cut edge of the shirt neckline. Cut a strip of ribbing to that length and 4" (10 cm) deep. Make sure the ribs are parallel to the 4" (10 cm) edge. Fold the strip in half lengthwise, right side out. Lay the shirt right side up and place the ribbing on top of the neckline, aligning the cut edges. Pin the pieces together.

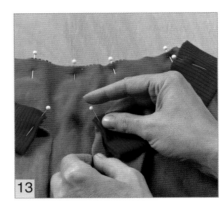

14 | Place the shirt in the serger with the ribbing on top. Sew the ribbing to the shirt with a 1/2" (1.3 cm) seam allowance. Gently press the ribbing away from the shirt, pressing the serged seam allowance toward the shirt.

15 | Measure the length of the front edge of the shirt from the fold of the bottom ribbing to the fold of the neck ribbing. Add 1" (2 cm) to that measurement. This number is the length of ribbing you'll need. Cut two strips of ribbing to that length and 5" (13 cm) deep. Fold each strip in half lengthwise, wrong side out. With a 1/2" (1 cm) seam allowance, serge both ends of each strip closed. Turn the strips right side out.

16 | Lay one of the shirt fronts right side up. Lay one of the ribbing strips on top, aligning the raw edges. Pin the pieces together. Repeat the process with the other shirt front and ribbing strip.

17 Place the shirt in the serger with the ribbing on top. Sew the ribbing strips to the shirt fronts with a $1/2$" (1.3 cm) seam allowance.

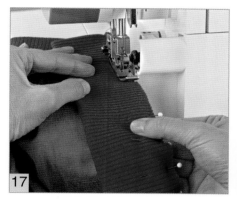

18 Measure around your arm at the point where the cuff ribbing will sit. Add 1" (2 cm) to this measurement. This number is the length of the ribbing you'll need. Cut two strips of ribbing to that length and 7" (17.5 cm) deep. Make sure the ribs are parallel to the 7" (17.5 cm) edge. Fold each strip in half so that the 7" (17.5 cm) edges meet. Serge these edges closed with a $1/2$" (1 cm) seam allowance, forming a tube.

19 To form the cuffs, fold the bottom of each tube up to meet the top, enclosing the seam.

20 With the sleeves right side out, slide a cuff, folded edge up, onto the bottom of each sleeve, aligning the raw edges and the seams. Pin the cuffs to the sleeve bottoms—stretch each cuff to fit its sleeve if you need to.

21 Turn the sleeves inside out. Place the pinned edge of one sleeve in the serger, with the ribbing on top. Sew the cuff to the sleeve. Repeat with the other sleeve.

22 If you'd like to add buttons, overlap the front ribbing bands. Mark the button positions as shown in the photo, page 44. Make corresponding marks inside the overlapped bands and sew snaps to these marks. Sew a button to the outside of the ribbing on top of each snap.

Make another cute cardigan from an oversized sweatshirt.

faux vintage sweater

Surprisingly easy to make, ruffles add a flirty charm that you'll be proud to say you designed yourself. You can create ruffles in any fabric you can think of to get the look you want. Try organza, satin, or even a whimsical print—just be sure the ruffle and cardigan fabrics can both be laundered the same way.

Machines and Feet

- 4- or 5-thread serger, with differential feed and rolled hem capability
- rolled hem foot (or plate, if needed for your serger)
- standard sewing machine with ballpoint needle

Materials

- cardigan (with or without a round yoke below the neckband)
- approximately $1/2$ yd. (0.5 m) contrasting fabric
- four spools of thread to match ruffles
- four spools of thread to match cardigan

Notions and Tools

- pins
- scissors
- ruler
- tape measure
- tailor's chalk
- tear-away stabilizer
- hand-sewing needle (optional)

Before

faux vintage sweater

1 Working with chalk or pins, mark a guideline for the lower edge of the ruffle, parallel to and 3" (7.5 cm) below the cardigan neckband. Measure the line, excluding the button band area on each front edge. Double this measurement and add 5" (13 cm).

This number is the total length of the fabric strip you'll need for your ruffle. If you want an extra-full ruffle, make the strip longer—stitch a sample first to determine how much longer, as explained in the sidebar at right.

2 Cut a strip that is 4" (10 cm) deep and the length you need for the ruffle. If you don't have enough fabric to cut the full length, cut more than one strip and sew the strips together with a standard 4-thread overlock stitch and matching thread. (Be sure to return the differential feed to normal if the serger is set for gathering.) Press the seam allowances to one side.

3 Set your serger for a 4-thread gathered overedge stitch, as described in the sidebar, testing and adjusting the differential feed to achieve the gathered effect you like. You can gather with a contrasting thread if you prefer.

getting ready to gather

To gather the ruffle, set your serger for the 3-thread or 4-thread overlock stitch (depending on your project) and adjust the differential feed control to its highest setting (the lowest setting will do the opposite—stretch the fabric). Sew along the edge of a sample strip of your fabric to see the effect. With differential feed, the overlock stitch becomes a gathered overedge stitch.

Experiment with the settings to get the right amount of ruffling for your project and to determine how much fabric you'll need. The fabric weight will affect how much the fabric will gather. To increase the fullness of the ruffle, increase the tension on the needle thread or try a longer stitch.

On some fabrics—like the silk dupioni used for this project—gathers stitched on the crosswise grain may require different tension settings than gathers stitched on the lengthwise grain. You'll get the best results working with medium- to lightweight fabrics. Experiment to find the effect you want for the project—but note the settings for each effect you like so you can re-create them all.

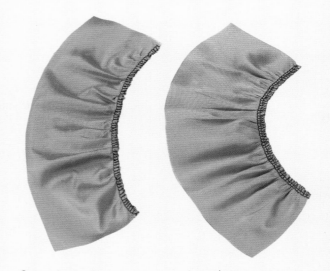

Crosswise grain   Lengthwise grain

4 Place the ruffle strip, right side up, in your serger and gather one long edge with a $1/2$" (1.3 cm) seam allowance. Turn the strip around and gather the other long edge the same way.

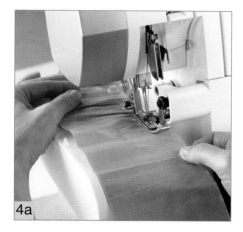

4a

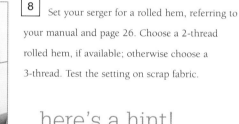

4b

5 Position the gathered strip on the cardigan, aligning the lower edge with the marked guideline. Pin the ruffle along the guideline, then pin the top edge just below the neckband. Evenly distribute and pin the extra fabric along the top edge of the ruffle. Trim any excess ruffle fabric next to the button area, leaving enough fabric to turn under a small hem. Turn under and pin the ends. If you like, you can hand-baste the gathered edges to the cardigan.

6 Try on the cardigan to see how far above the wrist you'd like to attach the sleeve ruffles. Mark the position with a pin or two. Remove the cardigan and lay one sleeve flat. Cut the sleeve $1/4$" (6 mm) below your mark. Work with the cut-off piece as a pattern to cut the other sleeve in the same manner.

7 Measure the circumference of the new sleeve edge. Double this amount and add 5" (13 cm). This number is the length of fabric you will need for the wrist ruffle. Adjust for extra fullness as you did for the neckline ruffle. Cut two fabric strips $2^{3}/4$" (7 cm) deep and the length you need for the sleeve ruffles.

8 Set your serger for a rolled hem, referring to your manual and page 26. Choose a 2-thread rolled hem, if available; otherwise choose a 3-thread. Test the setting on scrap fabric.

here's a hint!

If the hem stretches, increase the differential feed slightly or lengthen the stitch.

9 Working with a $1/2$" (1.3 cm) seam allowance, sew a rolled hem on the bottom edge of each sleeve ruffle strip.

9a

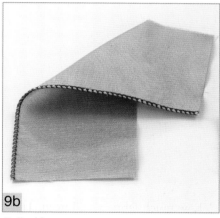

9b

Rolled hem

5

10 Reset your serger for the gathered overedge stitch. With a $1/2$" (1.3 cm) seam allowance and the strip right side up, gather the unhemmed edge of each sleeve ruffle.

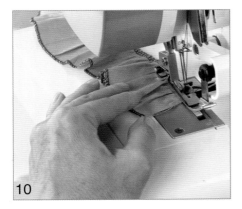

11 Cut each sleeve ruffle to the measurement of the sleeve bottom edge plus 1" (2 cm). Fold one ruffle in half, wrong side out, aligning the cut ends. With your sewing machine, stitch the ends together with a $1/2$" (1 cm) seam allowance. Join the ends of the other ruffle the same way.

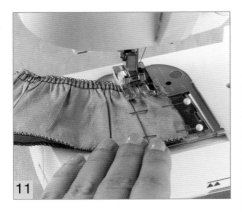

12 Rethread the serger with thread that matches the cardigan and reset it for the standard 4-thread overlock stitch. Taking care not to stretch the fabric, serge the bottom edge of each sleeve with a $1/4$" (6 mm) seam allowance.

13 With all the pieces right side out, slip a ruffle onto the bottom of each sleeve. Align the seams and overlap the ruffle on the sleeve so the gathers cover the serged edge. Pin the ruffles in place as shown in the phot, or hand-baste each ruffle to its sleeve.

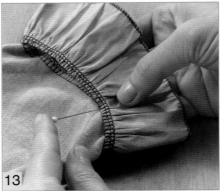

14 Cut pieces of tear-away stabilizer that are somewhat larger than the front and back of the neckline ruffle area. Pin the stabilizer to the inside of the cardigan, behind the ruffle, as shown in the photo. If you wish, you can cut narrow strips of stabilizer and pin them to the insides of the sleeves under the gathered edge of the ruffle.

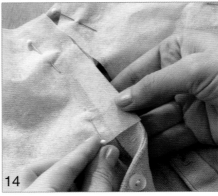

here's a hint!

Instead of pinning, adhere tear-away stabilizer with temporary basting spray. Just spray and finger-press.

15 Thread your sewing machine with top thread that matches the ruffle and bobbin thread that matches the cardigan. With the cardigan right side up, machine-sew the ruffles in place, stitching along the center of the gathered edge. If your sewing machine does not have a free arm, turn the sleeves inside out to sew on the sleeve ruffles.

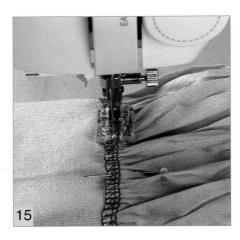

16 Remove the stabilizer and lightly steam-press the cardigan to shape.

To complete the makeover, replace the original buttons with new or vintage styles.

home décor

One of the fastest ways to update the look of a room is to change its accessories. Your serger will help you create home décor accents that have real style and a professional look—and are very easy to make! You can sew a blind hem for a curtain in no time. It's simple to make coordinating tiebacks to hold open the curtain panels, too.

Embellish small and simple accessories with serger stitches to add custom-designed decorator details. Try weaving ribbons through the flatlock stitch or create texture on a pillow with the cover stitch—or simply add a neat decorative edge to a length of a luscious fabric to make a cozy throw. Add a colorful flourish with your own wire-edged ribbons, which keep their shape prettily when tied.

cozy blanket
with overlock binding

Need a quick gift for a baby shower? Or a gift for yourself for those chilly nights? Make this super-quick throw blanket in any fun fabric you like and like the feel of. Simply cut the fabric to the size you want, cut round corners so you can serge all around, and then bind the edge with decorative thread and serger stitches. How easy is that?

Size
- 60" x 60" (152 x 152 cm), or any size desired

Machine
- 3-, 4-, or 5-thread serger with 3-thread overlock stitch capability

Materials
- a soft, cozy knit or woven fabric
- 12-wt. cotton thread
- two spools of rayon floss thread to match 12-wt. cotton thread

Notions and Tools
- bowl or plate for corner template
- pencil
- fabric marker
- measuring tape or long ruler
- scissors
- yarn needle or large tapestry needle

cozy blanket with overlock binding

1. Cut the fabric into a square or rectangle that is the finished size you want the blanket to be.

2. To plan the rounded corners, position an upside-down bowl or plate on each corner and draw around it with a fabric marker, as shown in the photo.

3. Cut all the corners along the marked lines.

4. Set your serger for a wide 3-thread overlock stitch, referring to your machine's manual. Make sure the needle is in the left position. Put the 12-wt. cotton thread in the needle and rayon floss in the upper and lower loopers. Test the settings on a scrap of the blanket fabric and adjust to get the effect you like.

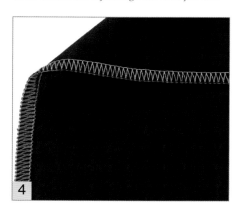

Wide 3-thread overlock

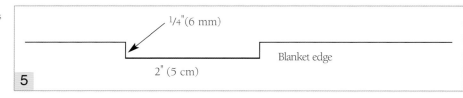

5. To prepare for binding the edge, cut a notch on one straight edge of the blanket. Make the notch $1/4$" (6 mm) deep and about 2" (5.1 cm) long, as shown in the drawing.

6. Gently pull the threads toward the back of the serger to remove the stitches from the stitch finger (page 11). Place the fabric right side up in the serger, with the notch under the presser foot. Position the fabric so the long edge of the notch is even with the cutting blade—when you start sewing, the blade will trim the fabric in line with the notch.

7. Hold the thread tails and begin to sew. After sewing several inches (centimeters), cut the thread tails close to the fabric.

8. Sew all the way around the blanket. When you stitch around the curves, guide the fabric slightly to the right in front of the presser foot. Watch the blade, not the needle, to keep the threads aligned with the cut edge.

9. As you reach the stitches in the notch, where you began, slow down. Carefully sew over the beginning stitches for about $1/2$" (1.3 cm), making sure not to cut them with the blade.

10. Raise the presser foot. Gently pull the fabric toward the back of the serger and then to the left, clearing the stitches from the stitch finger and moving the piece out from under the foot.

11 Lower the presser foot (make sure there's no fabric under it) and start sewing again to make a thread chain. Stop sewing and cut the thread chain, leaving a tail about 3" (8 cm) long attached to the blanket.

12 To secure the thread tail, thread it in the yarn needle and slide it for about 1" (2.5 cm) under the stitches on the wrong side of the blanket. Bring out the needle and clip off the excess thread tail close to where you exited.

Cuddle up on the
couch with your new
cozy throw!

reversible cover-stitch pillow

Why make another plain pillow when you can make this one? Ribbons, tassels, and decorative thread add sophisticated texture to even the most ordinary fabric. Experiment with your own stitch patterns and colors or just follow along with the choices here. These easy steps will teach you about what you can create with the versatile cover stitch.

Reverse side

Size
• 20" x 20" (51 x 51 cm)

Machines and Feet
• 5-thread serger with 3-needle cover-stitch capability, or cover-stitch machine
• standard sewing machine
• zipper foot

Materials
• 3/4 yd. (1 m) solid-color fabric, at least 45" (114 cm) wide
• 1 1/2 yd. (1.4 m) ribbon to complement the fabric, 3/8" (1 cm) wide
• four tassels
• two shank buttons, 1 1/8" (2.8 cm) in diameter (optional)
• three spools of 12-wt. cotton thread to contrast fabric
• one cone of serger thread to match 12-wt. cotton

• sewing thread to match fabric
• heavy-duty upholstery thread to match fabric

Notions and Tools
• fabric marker or chalk
• transparent grid ruler
• tear-away stabilizer (optional)
• scissors
• rotary cutter, ruler, and mat (optional)
• seam ripper
• loop turner or crochet hook
• 20" x 20" (51 x 51 cm) pillow form
• extra-long darning needle

Cutting List
• Cut four 11" (30 cm) squares solid-color fabric.
• Cut four 10 1/2" (28 cm) squares solid-color fabric.

reversible cover-stitch pillow

1 Set the serger for a 3-needle cover stitch, referring to your manual and Sewing Cover Stitch on page 38. Thread the needles with the 12-wt. cotton thread and thread the cover stitch looper with the serger thread. Practice the stitch if you are not familiar with it.

2 On two of the 11" (30 cm) fabric squares, working with a transparent grid ruler as a guide, draw a line 3" (8 cm) from and parallel to each edge. These are the ribbon placement lines.

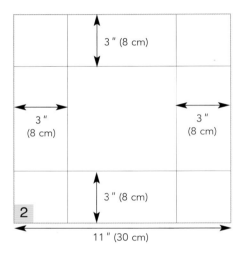

here's a hint!

If the fabric puckers as you sew, put tear-away stabilizer under it and try again.

3 On the same two squares, draw a line 2" (5.5 cm) from and parallel to each edge. These are the cover-stitch guidelines.

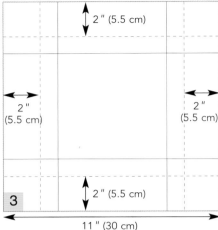

4 Cut eight 12" (31 cm) lengths of ribbon. Place one of the marked fabric squares in the serger, aligning the center needle with one of the marked ribbon guidelines. Center the ribbon over the line. Sew the ribbon to the fabric. (You can pin the ribbon if you like, but you don't need to.)

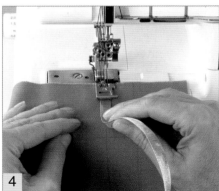

5 Rotate the square 90 degrees and sew on another piece of ribbon. Continue to sew ribbon on the two remaining guidelines and on the second marked fabric square.

6 Now sew cover stitch along each of the remaining marked guidelines on both squares. Align the center needle with the marked line as before, and rotate the square 90 degrees after sewing each line.

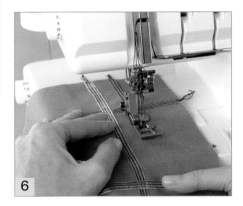

7 On each of the remaining 11" (30 cm) squares, draw a line across the middle. With the transparent grid ruler as a guide, draw three parallel lines on each side of this line, placing them at 1¹/₄" (3.5 cm) intervals.

lines 1¹/₄" (3.5 cm) apart

If your presser foot has a slot in front of the needle, thread the ribbon through the slot and under the foot before beginning to sew. If not, simply place the ribbon under the presser foot.

8 In the same way, draw lines that are perpendicular to the first set, to create a grid.

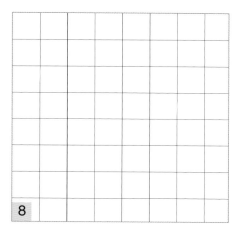

9 Sew cover stitch over each marked line, aligning the center needle with the line.

10 Trim each embellished square to measure 10¹/₂" (28 cm) square. Be sure to center the embellished portion.

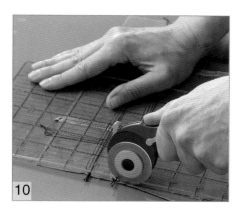

11 Thread your standard sewing machine with thread to match the fabric and set it to a medium straight stitch. With the right sides together and a ¹/₄" (1 cm) seam allowance, sew one of the embellished squares to one of the plain squares along one edge. Repeat to sew together pairs of the remaining embellished and plain squares. Press open all the seam allowances.

12 Now you'll join the pillow sections in a checkerboard fashion. Place two of the pieces right sides together, arranging them so each ribbon-embellished square faces a plain square. Sew them together along one long edge with a ¹/₄" (6 mm) seam allowance. Join the remaining two pieces in the same way. Press open all the seam allowances.

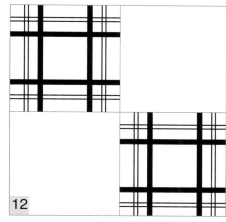

13 Place the two checkerboard sections right sides together, aligning all the edges. Sew together along all edges with a ¹/₄" (1 cm) seam allowance, leaving a 14" (36 cm) opening along one edge so you can insert the pillow form later.

14 Place the zipper foot on the machine, to the right of the needle. Working with a seam ripper, cut one stitch at each corner of the pillow cover. Slip one of the tassels inside the cover. Then insert the loop turner, grab the tassel loop with the turner, and pull it through the opening created by the cut stitch, as shown in the photo. Pull the tassel snug against the corner and remove the loop turner.

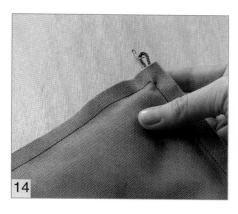

15 Sew across the corner seam allowance a few times to secure the tassel loop and then sew around the corner to close the seamline again. Insert and sew a tassel at each of the other corners in the same way.

16 Turn the pillow cover right side out through the opening. Insert the pillow form. Fold the seam allowances along the opening to the inside. Neatly hand-sew the opening closed.

17 With upholstery thread and a long darning needle, sew a button to the center of each side of the pillow. Pull the needle all the way through the pillow as you stitch, passing it through each button in turn and pulling the thread taut to create a slight depression in the pillow surface.

Make a different style for every room in the house.

wire-edged ribbon bow

No more floppy ribbons! With your serger, you can quickly hem strips of fabric to make your own ribbons—for wreaths, hats, packages, or whatever else you'd like to embellish with a bow! The secret? You simply enclose a length of wire in the rolled hems so the edges will hold their shape however you decide to arrange them. Change the fabric quantities and make as much ribbon as you like, in any width. This bow is for a wreath.

Size
- 2$\frac{1}{2}$" x 90" (6.3 x 228 cm), or any length desired

Machines and Feet
- 3-, 4-, or 5-thread serger, with rolled hem capability
- yarn application foot
- standard sewing machine

Materials
- $\frac{1}{2}$ yd. (0.5 m) fabric
- $\frac{1}{2}$ yd. (0.5 m) fusible webbing
- rayon floss or Pearl Crown Rayon to match or contrast with fabric
- two cones of all-purpose thread to match the rayon floss
- 32-gauge wire, at least 100" (254 cm) long
- florist wire (18" [0.5 cm] piece)
- wreath

Notions and Tools
- scissors
- wire cutters
- liquid seam sealant

Cutting List
- Cut two 6" x 45" (15 x 114 cm) strips of fabric.
- Cut enough 3" (7.5 cm)-wide strips from the fusible webbing to total 90" (228 cm) in length.

wire-edged ribbon bow

1 With your sewing machine, sew the strips of fabric together to make one long strip. Press open the seam allowances.

2 Lay the strip wrong side up on your ironing board. Position one piece of fusible webbing, paper side up, on top, aligning one edge of it with one edge of the fabric. Follow the package directions to fuse the webbing to the fabric.

3 Fuse the rest of the webbing to the rest of the strip in the same way. Remove the paper backing from all the webbing.

4 Fold the fabric in half lengthwise, enclosing the webbing. Fuse together the layers.

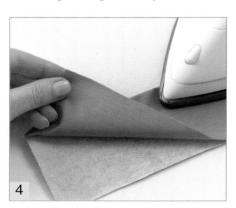

here's a hint!

If your fabric is heavy and stiff, you won't need to double it or reinforce it with fusible webbing.

5 Set your serger for a 3-thread rolled hem, referring to your manual and page 26. Attach the yarn application foot. Place the rayon floss in the upper looper and the all-purpose thread in the needle and lower looper. Test the setting on a scrap of fabric.

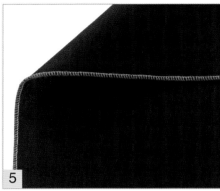

3-thread rolled hem

6 Thread the 32-gauge wire into the slot of the presser foot, bringing the end of the wire through the foot and extending it out the back.

7 Position one end of the fabric strip under the presser foot, aligning the long edge $1/4"$ (6 mm) to the right of the blade. Serge a rolled hem along the entire length of the ribbon, feeding the wire through the foot and into the hem as you go.

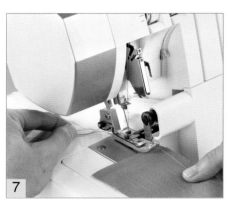

8 When you reach the end of the fabric, continue to serge over the wire for a short distance. With the wire cutters, cut the excess wire right at the end of the strip. Cut the thread chain with scissors, if necessary.

9 In the same way, serge a wired hem on the other long edge of the strip. Be sure to have the same side of the fabric facing up as before.

10 Tie a florist-style bow, following the instructions in the sidebar at right.

11 Wrap the ends of the florist wire around the wreath and twist them to secure. Cut off any excess. Arrange the loops of the bow. Arrange the tails too, trimming the ends into points if you'd like. Seal the ends of the stitched edges with a drop of seam sealant. Seal the cut ends of the ribbon, too, so the fabric doesn't fray.

Why not make another pretty bow to wear—
a small one for a jacket or hat!

tying the bow

Form two loops near one end of the ribbon, extending the tail. Loop the ribbon over and behind the first loop. Then, twisting as you go to keep the same side out and pinching at the center, continue to loop the ribbon back and forth behind the first loops. Stop when the remaining ribbon is not long enough to form another loop or when the bow is the desired size.

Pass the florist's wire through the first loop; fold the wire in half over all the layers. Twist tightly to secure the bow.

more bows!

Once you've mastered this technique, you'll be able to make large fabric ribbons in any color or pattern to decorate seasonal wreaths for your door or mantel. It's fun to make smaller ones, too, to decorate gift packages with an extra-special touch. Tie a simple bow around the handle of a small basket filled with flowers, and you have a decorative centerpiece or sweet flower-girl bouquet. Experiment with different thread textures and different fabric widths to create a variety of effects. Try working with two different colors of fabric, too, fusing them together to make a double-faced ribbon—it will tie into an intriguing, multicolor bow.

ribbon-trimmed table runner

This elegant runner makes a beautiful accent for your table. The special decorative touch is the ribbon woven through the flatlock stitching joining the fabric pieces. Change the style from formal to casual and experiment with bright, bold colors or soft, subtle shades.

Size

- approximately 16" x 55$^{1}/_{2}$" (41 x 141 cm)

Machines

- 3-, 4-, or 5-thread serger, with 2-thread flatlock stitch capability
- standard sewing machine

Materials

- $^{1}/_{4}$ yd. (0.25 m) each of two coordinating cotton fabrics, for border
- 1$^{1}/_{2}$ yd. (1.5 m) cotton fabric, for center of runner
- 1$^{3}/_{4}$ yd. (1.75 m) cotton fabric, for backing
- one spool 30-wt. cotton thread to match one of the two coordinating fabrics
- one cone of serger thread, to match the 30-wt. cotton thread
- one cone of all-purpose thread to match the 30-wt. cotton thread
- 8 yd. (7.5 m) satin ribbon, $^{1}/_{8}$" to $^{1}/_{4}$" (3 to 6 mm) wide
- four large beads and four coordinating seed beads, to decorate corners (optional)

Notions and Tools

- scissors
- tape measure
- rotary cutter, ruler, and mat
- yarn needle or large tapestry needle
- bead needle

Cutting List

- Cut two 3" x 44" (7.5 x 112 cm) strips from each of the coordinating fabrics.
- Cut one 17" x 56" (43 x 142 cm) strip from the backing fabric.
- Cut one 11$^{1}/_{2}$" x 50$^{3}/_{4}$" (29 x 129 cm) strip from the center fabric.

Note: If your serger does not sew a 2-thread flatlock stitch, you may use a 3-thread flatlock stitch instead. For this stitch, you will need two cones of sewing thread to match the 30-wt. cotton thread.

ribbon-trimmed table runner

1 Set the serger for a wide, 2-thread flatlock stitch, referring to your machine's manual. If you don't have the 2-thread option on your machine, set it for a 3-thread flatlock stitch. Make sure the needle is in the left position. Put the 30-wt. cotton thread in the needle and the serger thread in the lower looper. For a 3-thread flatlock stitch, put serger thread in both loopers.

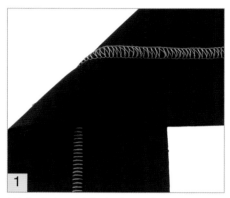

Wide 2-thread flatlock stitch

2 Lay the 3" (7.5 cm)-wide fabric strips on your serger table, keeping the two colors separate. Place two different-color strips right sides together, aligning all the edges. Serge these strips together along one long edge. Trim off any fraying threads, but don't cut away any of the fabric.

3 Join the remaining strips to each other in the same way. Then serge the pairs of strips together along one long edge, making sure the colors alternate.

4 Gently pull the fabric strips apart along each seam so that the enclosed seam allowances shift and overlap and the stitches form a ladder over them.

5 Press the joined strips so they make a flat block of fabric.

6 Cut a 4' (1.2 m) length of ribbon. Thread it onto the yarn needle. Insert the needle under two thread "rungs" on one of the flatlock seams. Then pass it over the next two rungs and under the following two rungs. Continue to weave the ribbon through the stitches in this way, gently pulling it flat every once in a while.

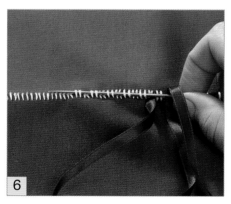

7 Weave a piece of ribbon through each remaining flatlock seam. Press the block so it lies flat again.

8 Lay the block on the cutting mat so that the strips are perpendicular to the left edge of the mat. With the rotary cutter and ruler, trim away any uneven edges and ribbon ends to straighten the left edge of the block.

9 Working with the ruler as a guide, cut a 3" (7.5 cm) strip from the left end of the block. Continue to cut the block into a total of twelve 3" (7.5 cm) strips.

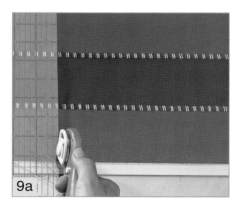

10 Making sure the colors alternate, serge three of the strips together to make a strip with twelve squares. Repeat with three more strips. Flatten the new seams and weave ribbon through them. You now have two long strips and two short ones.

11 Lay the table runner center right side up on your work surface. With the right sides up, position the short border strips alongside each end and the long border strips alongside the long edges. Make sure the colors alternate all the way around. If they don't, rotate the strips until they do.

12 With the right sides together, pin and serge each short border strip to the center panel. Flatten the seams and weave ribbon through them.

13 Making sure to keep the alternating color sequence, serge each long border to the center panel. Be sure to center each border along the edge of the center panel. Flatten the seams and weave ribbon through them. Press the runner top. If there are any uneven edges, trim them so the piece is a rectangle.

14 Lay the runner backing on your work surface, right side up. Lay the runner top right side down on top of it, aligning all the edges. If the backing is larger than the top, slide the cutting mat under it and, working with the ruler as a guide, cut off the excess. Pin the two layers together along the edges.

15 Thread your standard sewing machine with the all-purpose thread and set it to a medium straight stitch. With a $1/4"$ (1 cm) seam allowance, sew the top to the back along all edges. Leave an opening about 6" (15 cm) long along one edge for turning.

16 Trim the seam allowance at the runner corners. Turn the runner right side out through the opening. Fold in the seam allowances along the opening and neatly sew it closed by hand.

To add sparkle and style, hand-sew a large bead and a seed bead to each corner.

simple curtains

Curtains can really make the room! They also give you with the perfect chance to work with lots of beautiful fabric and trim. These full-length curtains with clip-on rings are so quick and simple to make, you may want to make several pairs in different fabrics and change them with the seasons—or with your mood! You can let the curtains hang just as they are or make the contrasting tieback bands on page 78 to gracefully hold them open.

Size (each panel)
- approximately 51" x 60" (129 x 153 cm)

Machines
- 3-, 4-, or 5-thread serger (to sew 3-thread overlock stitch)
- blind-hem foot
- standard sewing machine

Materials
- 4 yd. (3.65 m) decorator fabric (at least 54" [137 cm] wide)
- 4 yd. (3.65 m) tassel fringe or other decorative trim
- three cones of serger thread to match fabric
- all-purpose thread to match fabric and trim
- curtain rod and clip-on rings

Notions and Tools
- scissors
- pins
- yarn needle
- seam gauge

Cutting List
- Cut two panels from the decorator fabric, each 53" x 70" (134 x 178 cm). (Trim off both of the selvages.)

Note: For information on how to measure your specific window, consult the *SINGER Simple Home Décor Handbook* or another reference. Be sure to buy enough fabric so that you have scraps for testing the stitching techniques.

simple curtains

1 Place one of the curtain panels wrong side up on your ironing board, with the bottom edge on the surface of the board. Working with the seam gauge, fold up a 2$^{1}/_{2}$" (6.5 cm)-deep hem across the bottom, pressing as you go. Pin the hem in place, positioning pinheads away from the hem. Pin the second panel the same way.

2 Set your serger for a narrow 3-thread overlock stitch, referring to your machine's manual. Set the needle in the right-hand position and select the longest possible stitch length. Put the blind-hem foot on the serger.

3 Serge a blind hem at the bottom of each panel, following the instructions in the sidebar on the facing page.

5 Serge a blind hem on each side edge. Secure the thread tails by threading each tail in the yarn needle and then sliding it under the stitches on the wrong side of the hem (page 15).

6 For the top hem, fold up and press 2$^{1}/_{2}$" (6.5 cm) to the wrong side at the top of one panel. Fold this hem up and press again. Pin the hem in place. Repeat for the second panel.

7 Thread your standard sewing machine with thread to match the fabric and set it to a medium straight stitch. Place one of the panels wrong side up in the machine, with the hem extending to the right of the needle. Sew the hem, stitching close to the inside fold. Sew the hem on the second panel the same way.

9 Sew the trim in place with a long straight stitch on your standard machine. Stitch close to both edges of the trim. If the middle of the trim is raised, adjust the needle position or change to the zipper foot—whichever allows you to feed the trim evenly under the foot and stitch near the edge.

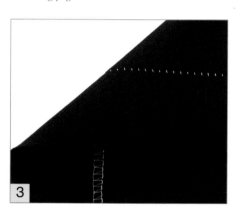

Blind hem

4 To prepare the side hems, fold up 1$^{1}/_{4}$" (3 cm) of fabric on each vertical edge of both panels, pressing and pinning as before.

8 Cut two pieces of the tassel trim, each the length of the curtain panels plus 1" (3 cm). Lay one of the panels right side up and pin a piece of trim along the left edge, tucking under $^{1}/_{2}$" (1.5 cm) at top and bottom edges. Pin the other piece of trim to the right edge of the second panel.

10 Attach clip-on rings to the top of each panel, spacing them evenly. Slide the rings over the curtain rod, making sure the trimmed edges of the panels meet in the middle of the rod. Mount the rod on its wall brackets. Adjust the fullness of the panels so the fabric is evenly distributed at each end of the window.

blind hemming

Before you stitch your project, test the blind-hem technique. Fold up and press a hem to the wrong side along one edge of scrap fabric. It doesn't matter how deep the hem is as long as it isn't tiny. Pin the hem in place, positioning the pinheads away from the fold, as shown in top photo.

Turn the scrap right side up, placing the hem to your left. Lift the right edge of the fabric, and fold it over so it lies flat on top of the hem. The cut edge of the hem should extend about 1/4" (6 mm), as shown in the center photo.

Transfer the fabric to your serger, without changing the orientation (the now-covered hem should still be to your left). Feed the fabric under the presser foot, aligning it so the needle barely pierces the fold and the overedge stitches fall on the extending fabric. Align the fold with the guide on the front of the foot. Sew, removing the pins as you go.

After you've sewn several inches (centimeters), unfold the stitched hem and look at the right side of the fabric. The stitches should barely show. The front guide on most blind-hem feet is adjustable, so if your stitches are too visible or are not catching the fold, check your manual to see how to make the needed adjustment. The weight of the fabric may affect the results, too, so don't be surprised if your first test isn't perfect.

For more pizzazz,
add trim to both vertical
edges and along the
hem, too.

curtain tiebacks

Curtain tiebacks add a simple but effective finishing touch—and they are functional, too. Tiebacks in coordinating fabrics, like these, look like a graceful sash. Just by releasing or securing them, you can quickly open and close your curtains—for privacy at night and more sunlight during the day. Experiment to see how high above the sill to install them.

Size (each tieback)
• 3" x 26" (7.5 x 66 cm)

Machines and Feet
• 4- or 5-thread serger (to sew 4-thread overlock stitch)
• cording foot
• standard sewing machine

Materials
• 1/4 yd. (0.25 m) decorator fabric, 54" (137 cm) wide, for tieback
• 1/8 yd. (12 cm) contrasting fabric for piping
• 3 yd. (2.7 m) thin cotton filler cord
• four cones of serger thread to match piping fabric

Notions and Tools
• scissors
• four small plastic rings, about 1/2" (1.3 cm) in diameter
• hand-sewing needle
• yarn needle
• two cup hooks (to mount to the wall)

Cutting List
• Cut four 3 1/2" x 27" (9 x 68 cm) strips of tieback fabric.
• Cut four 1 1/2" x 27" (3.5 x 68 cm) strips of the contrasting fabric.
• Cut four 26" (66 cm) pieces of filler cord.

curtain tiebacks

1 At the end of each small strip of contrasting fabric, fold and press $1/2$" (1 cm) to the wrong side.

2 Set your serger for the 4-thread overlock stitch, referring to your machine's manual. Adjust all the thread tensions to their normal setting. Put the cording foot on the serger. Practice the technique, following the instructions in the sidebar at right. Then make four pieces of piping with the filler cord and the small strips of contrasting fabric.

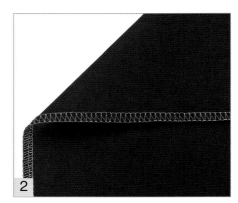

4-thread overlock stitch

3 Lay one of the tieback strips right side up. Place a piece of piping on top of it, along the right-hand edge. Position the piping so the serged edge aligns with the cut edge of the strip and the strip extends $1/2$" (1 cm) beyond the piping at each end, as shown in the photo.

4 Lay a second large fabric strip face down on top of the strip with the piping. Make sure all the edges align. Pin through all layers along the edge where the piping is positioned. Pin a piece of piping between each of the remaining large fabric strips in the same way.

5 Serge the pinned layers together on the piped edge of each tieback, feeding the piping under the groove in the cording foot.

6 In the same way, pin a piece of piping between the layers on the remaining long (open) edge of each tieback. Serge these edges. Each tieback is now a tube.

7 Turn the tiebacks right side out.

8 Tuck the fabric at the open ends of each between the layers. Neatly sew the open ends closed by hand. On one side of each tieback, sew a small plastic ring close to each end.

9 Install a cup hook on the wall on each side of the window, at the same distance from the floor for each side. Wrap each tieback around a curtain panel and slip the plastic rings into the cup hooks. Adjust the fullness of the curtains inside the tiebacks.

Change the fabric and make yourself a belt!
Attach ribbons to the end and
tie them through the ring.

prepping for piping

Cut fabric strips to the dimensions you need for your project. You can cut them on the straight grain or on the bias (page 31). Bias piping will lie along a curved edge more easily than straight-grain piping.

To make a sample of the piping, cut a fabric strip 1$\frac{1}{2}$" (3.5 cm) wide and 12" (30 cm) long. Cut a piece of filler cord 12" (30 cm) long. Lay the fabric wrong side up. Center the cord on the fabric, then fold the fabric over the cord, bringing together the long fabric edges. Hold this "sandwich" with the folded edge and cord to the left, the open edges to the right as shown in the top photo.

Position the strip in the serger, placing the cord under the groove in the bottom of the cording foot. The open edges of the strip should extend to the right of the foot.

Start stitching. The serger blade will automatically trim away the extra seam allowance, and the seam will hold the cord snug inside the folded strip. Sew to the end of the strip.

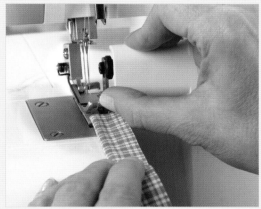

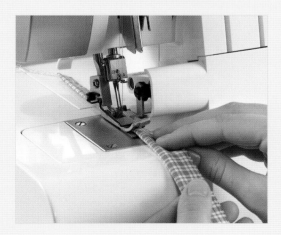

fashions and accessories

A serger makes it extra easy for you to step out in style. It's the perfect companion for your sewing machine. It stitches and trims seam allowances all with one pass—so sewing is faster than with a standard machine alone. The serger also offers a variety of specialty stitches that are not only useful, but lovely to look at, too.

In this chapter, you'll learn how to make a quick-to-sew, flirty peasant skirt with gathers and a classy lightweight wrap with fringe. You'll also find fun accents—a wraparound belt with leather cord ties, dangling tassel trims, and vintage-style rosettes. There so many choices—the hardest part will be deciding which to make first!

thread-chain tassel

Here's a project that's so easy that even someone who has never sewn a stitch before can make it perfectly—first time out! You create the tassel "yarn" simply by serging a chain of stitches. All you need is your serger, some spools of thread, and a little time. So put on some good music and sit down to serge a very long rolled hem—without the fabric!

Machine and Feet
- 3-, 4-, or 5-thread serger with rolled hem capability
- rolled hem foot (or plate, if needed for your serger)

Materials
- one spool of novelty thread, such as Pearl Crown Rayon
- two spools of all-purpose thread to match novelty thread
- $1/4$ yd. (23 cm) narrow ribbon, for hanging loop
- forty small (size 6°) rocaille beads or as many as desired (optional)

Notions and Tools
- $5^1/2$" x $6^1/2$" (14 x 16.5 cm) piece heavyweight cardboard
- scissors
- yarn needle or large tapestry needle
- seam sealant
- small steel crochet hook (size 9/1.25 mm), for beads

thread-chain tassel

1   Set your serger for a narrow 3-thread rolled hem, referring to your machine's manual and page 26. Put novelty thread in the upper looper and all-purpose thread in the needle and lower looper.

2   Lower the presser foot. Hold the thread tails in your left hand and begin to sew. Keep the machine at a moderate, steady speed. Adjusting your left hand as needed, gently hold onto the thread chain as it emerges behind the presser foot.

3   The thread chain should look like a loosely twisted novelty yarn. Adjust the stitch length and thread tension and sew to test the settings until you get the look you want.

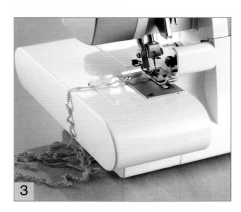

4   Continue to make "yarn" on the serger until you have about 25 to 30 yd. (23 to 28 m). Cut off a 12" (30.5 cm) piece and set it aside.

here's a hint!

Stop serging every so often and wrap the "yarn" into a ball to prevent twisting, tangling, and knotting.

5   Wrap the yarn lengthwise around the cardboard, as shown in the photo.

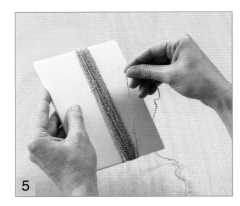

6   Continue until you've wrapped the cardboard 70 or 80 times. Cut off any extra yarn and tuck the end under the wraps. Slide the ribbon under the wraps at one edge of the cardboard.

7   Pull the ribbon through and bring the ends together above the cardboard. Tie the ribbon in a secure knot.

8   Cut the yarn wraps at the end of the cardboard opposite the ribbon. Remove the cardboard.

9   Hold the tassel by the ribbon and smooth the yarns so they hang straight. Then tie the reserved 12" (30.5 cm) piece of yarn around the tassel, about ¾" (2 cm) below the ribbon. Tightly wrap the tied yarn around the top of the tassel several times, as shown in the photo.

10   Thread the ends of the wrapped yarn in the yarn needle and insert it behind the wraps. Pull the yarn end through and tug to secure. Trim off any extending ends.

How fun is this? Experiment with textures and colors to make tassels to dangle anywhere!

11 If you'd like, you can add a bead to the end of some of the yarns. Just slide the bead onto the crochet hook and insert the hook through the thread chain as shown in the photo. Slide the bead off the hook and onto the yarn.

12 Slide the bead a bit further up the yarn to position it. Then put a drop of seam sealant on the strand at each end of the bead to secure the bead to the yarn. Let the sealant dry. Repeat this process to add as many beads as you'd like.

13 Tie the tassel to your project. You can also attach it by inserting the ribbon ends in a seam.

here's a hint!

If you can't easily slide the ribbon under the wrapped "yarn," thread it in the yarn needle and slide the needle under the yarn.

more tassels!

Tassels are a lot of fun to make. And there are so many novelty threads and so many colors to choose from, you can really go to town!

Make two and add them to the end of a tie belt, or make four and sew them to the corners of a shawl or poncho. They make great trims for home accessories, too—as shade pulls or dangles on drawer pulls, the flap of a tote, or even the ends of curtain tiebacks! Add tassels to gift wrap or make one-of-a-kind key chains or stocking stuffers for all your friends.

You can make any size tassel you like. Just change the size of the cardboard piece you use for wrapping and make more or less of your custom-made chain yarn.

Work with more than one color of "yarn" to create a multicolored tassel (top photo below). Or use contrasting novelty and all-purpose threads. Add beads of all sizes, colors, and material—let your imagination lead the way!

fringed wrap

For a wrap with class, start with just a plain square of soft, pretty fabric. Working with your serger, you'll embellish it with parallel bands of decorative flatlock stitching. It's easy to stitch the bands: Fold the fabric, stitch along the fold, and then gently pull the fabric so it lies flat again. To finish, you'll create a feathery fringe on the edges. A lovely look that couldn't be easier!

Size

- 53" x 53" (135 x 135 cm) with fringe, or size desired

Machine

- 3-, 4-, or 5-thread serger with 3-thread flatlock stitch capability

Materials

- 1 1/4 yd. (1.4 m) loosely woven fabric, at least as wide as the desired width of wrap including fringe
- two spools of Pearl Crown Rayon thread in color to complement fabric, or other decorative thread
- four spools of all-purpose thread to match decorative thread

Notions and Tools

- transparent quilter's or grid ruler
- fabric marker
- T-pin or other large straight pin
- yarn needle or tapestry needle
- liquid seam sealant

Note: The flatlock stitch requires one spool of Pearl Crown Rayon and two spools of all-purpose thread. You'll need extra of each, however, to sew all those rows of flatlock without running out of thread!

fringed wrap

1 Set your serger for a 3-thread flatlock stitch, referring to your machine's manual and the sidebar at right. Practice the technique on a scrap of fabric.

3-thread flatlock stitch

2 Decide the dimensions of your wrap and cut the fabric to that size. Be sure the cut edges of the wrap follow the straight grain of the fabric (page 31). Cut off the selvages if using the full fabric width.

3 Lay the fabric flat right side up on your work surface. Working with the transparent ruler and a fabric marker, measure and mark a line along one edge, $1^1/2$" (4 cm) from the cut edge.

4 Measure and mark another line $1^1/2$" (4 cm) from the first one (3" [8 cm] from the cut edge). Then measure and mark a third line $1^1/2$" (4 cm) from the second one ($4^1/2$" [12 cm] from the edge).

5 In the same way, measure and mark three lines parallel to the other edges of the fabric. Be sure to mark along the full length of each edge so the lines cross at the corners.

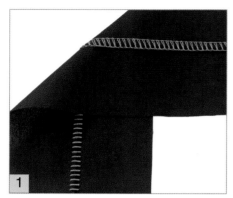

6 Make a dot at each corner to mark the intersection of the lines that are $1^1/2$" (4 cm) from the cut edge.

7 Place the marked fabric wrong side up on the ironing board, with one cut edge at the front of the board. Fold up the edge along the line marked $4^1/2$" (12 cm) from the cut edge and press the fold.

8 Place the fabric in the serger with the fold aligned for flatlocking. Stitch all the way along the folded edge.

9 Unfold the fabric so it lies flat inside the stitches. Press from the wrong side.

10 Repeat steps 7, 8, and 9 on the edge that is opposite the one you just stitched. Then flatlock the two remaining edges in the same way.

11 Flatlock the middle marked line in the same way—folding, stitching, unfolding, and pressing on two opposite edges and then on the two remaining edges.

flatlock stitching on a fold

Set your serger for a wide 3-thread flatlock stitch. Disengage the blade. Put decorative thread in the upper looper. Put all-purpose thread in the needle and lower looper.

To test this technique, mark a line on the right side of the fabric where you want the stitches to be, at least 1" (2.5 cm) from the cut edge. Mark all the way across the fabric. Fold the fabric on the line (keep it right side out) and press the fold. Place the fabric under the presser foot with the needle about 1/4" (6 mm) from the edge of the fold.

Begin to sew, stitching slowly. Make sure the fold aligns with the middle of the band of stitches—they should extend beyond it, as shown in the top two photos.

Sew to the end of the fold and remove the fabric from the serger. Gently pull the fabric along the stitched area so that it unfolds and lies flat inside the stitches, as shown in the third photo. Gently press the fabric from the wrong side.

Adjust the thread tension to change the decorative effect if you wish (page 18). Keep practicing until you feel you're in control of the stitching.

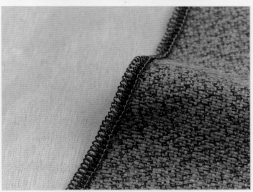

fringed wrap

12 Now flatlock along one of the lines marked 1¹/₂" (4 cm) from the cut edge but, this time, start stitching at the dot that marks the intersecting line. Stop stitching when you reach the next dot. To remove the fabric from the serger, lift the presser foot and pull the fabric away from the foot toward the back, pinching the stitches to keep them intact and working the handwheel back and forward as you pull.

13 Flatten the fold and press the stitches. Pull the threads from this last band of stitching to the wrong side of the fabric. Working with the yarn needle, weave the threads under the flatlock stitches for about 1" (2.5 cm) and cut off the excess (page 15).

14 Repeat steps 12 and 13 on the remaining edges of the fabric.

15 At each corner, use a pin to carefully undo the flatlock stitches that cross the 1¹/₂" (4 cm) deep margin, stopping when you reach the intersecting band of stitches.

16 Pull all the thread ends to the wrong side. With the yarn needle, weave each set under the flatlock stitches and cut off the excess.

17 To fringe the edges, lay the wrap flat. Pull out the threads parallel to the edge that's closest to you. Starting at the right end of the cut edge, loosen the first thread, working with the tip of the T-pin or yarn needle to work the thread free. Gently pull it out and work it free along the entire edge. Continue removing all the threads on this edge this way, one at a time, until you reach the band of flatlock stitches. Fringe each edge in turn, rotating the wrap as you work.

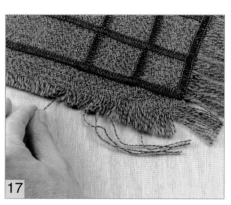

18 To secure the stitches, put a drop of seam sealant at the ends of the bands of stitches on the wrong side of the wrap. Let the sealant dry.

here's a hint!

If your fabric does not feed smoothly through the serger, check the stitch length. It may be too short for the fabric.

Wrap and go—how many of these can you fit in your closet?

rolled rosettes

Oh, what a rolled hem can do! That's all you need to make the luscious rosettes on this evening clutch bag. Texturized nylon thread creates a well-defined edge finish on the bias-cut fabric strips. Then you just gather and roll the strips to make the blossoms. Choose a satiny fabric with lots of sheen and color to make the most of the sculptural shape.

Machine and Feet

- 3-, 4-, or 5-thread serger, with differential feed and rolled hem capability
- rolled hem foot or plate (if needed for your serger)

Materials

- 1³/4" x 33" (4.5 x 84 cm) bias strip of fabric (for one rosette)
- one spool of texturized nylon thread to match rosette fabric
- two spools of all-purpose thread to match texturized nylon thread

Notions and Tools

- ruler
- fabric marker
- scissors
- hand-sewing needle

rolled rosettes

1 | Cut a 1³/₄" x 33" (4 x 84 cm) bias strip of fabric for each rosette you would like to make (page 31).

2 | Set your serger for a narrow, 3-thread rolled hem, referring to your machine's manual and page 26. Put texturized nylon thread in the upper looper and all-purpose thread in the needle and lower looper. Test the setting on a scrap of fabric.

3-thread rolled hem

3 | Sew a rolled hem on one long edge of the bias strip. Taper the strip at one end.

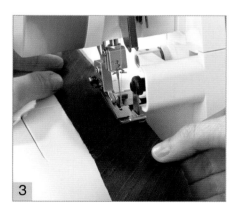

4 | Reset your serger for a gathered overedge stitch (3-thread overlock stitch with differential feed), referring to your machine's manual and page 11. Adjust the differential feed control to achieve the tightest gathering possible. Test the gathering technique on a piece of scrap fabric, following the sidebar on page 52.

5 | Gather the unhemmed long edge of the bias strip.

6 | To form the rosette, follow the sequence shown in the photos below. Roll up the bias strip, beginning at the tapered end. Sew the gathered edges together by hand as you roll. Turn the rosette right side up from time to time to see that it flares prettily.

7 When you've finished rolling the rosette, make a few stitches across the bottom to secure it.

8 Hand-stitch the rosette to your project. Stitch through the bottom of the rosette in several places to make sure it sits snugly and securely.

here's a hint!

When making more than one rosette, complete each step on each strip before going on to the next step.

Make one or more rosettes of any size you like—tiny ones are sweet and large ones are dramatic.

more rosettes!

What's on your calendar? A prom, a wedding, a holiday celebration? One or more well-placed rosettes dress up clothes or accessories for any occasion. Choose a dressy fabric, something with sheen or a little metallic glimmer. Looking for something a little more casual? Try a fun cotton print, lightweight denim, or even thin, colorful felt!

Sheer fabric makes a delicate bloom, like the one shown here. You can finish it with a matching hem or a contrasting hem to emphasize the shapes.

If you want to create a more intricate rosette, place two different-color strips back to back. Then hem, roll, and stitch them as one.

hip belt

This wide, embellished belt has a tie closure made of leather cords. The cords are simple to attach with the beading foot and flatlock stitch. The fabric surface of the belt is embellished with perpendicular rows of chain stitching. Keep the colors subtle and low-key, as in this project—or get a little wild with decorative threads and colors. Either way, this hip belt sits nicely at your waist or hips.

Size
- length and width as desired

Machines and Feet
- 5-thread serger, with 2-thread flatlock and chain stitch capabilities
- beading foot
- standard sewing machine, with a needle appropriate for your fabric and a size 16 needle or leather needle

Materials
- sturdy fabric (linen or denim), one piece 20" (51 cm) deep and wide enough to fit around your waist or hips
- three spools of topstitching thread or buttonhole twist to contrast with fabric
- one spool of all-purpose thread to match topstitching thread
- one spool of all-purpose thread to match fabric
- 5 yd. (5 m) slender braided leather cord, for ties
- six beads to fit onto cord ends (optional)

Notions and Tools
- tape measure
- 45-degree triangle or ruler with 45-degree marking
- transparent grid ruler
- scissors
- fabric marker
- pins
- hand-sewing needle

Seam Allowance
- 1/4" (6 mm)

Cutting List
Fabric
- Cut one belt back 5" (12.5 cm) deep x hip-measurement-minus-9" (23 cm) wide.
- Cut one belt back lining 4$^{1}/_{2}$" (11 cm) deep x hip-measurement-minus-10" (25.5 cm) wide.
- Cut two belt fronts, each 4$^{1}/_{2}$" (11 cm) deep x 10" (25.5 cm) wide.

Leather cord
- Cut six 30" (76 cm) pieces.

hip belt

1 Measure your waist or hips, depending on where you want to wear the belt. Cut the pieces, referring to the cutting list for sizes. If your fabric ravels easily, finish the edges of each piece with a 3-thread overlock stitch—be sure not to cut off any of the fabric.

2 Set your serger for chain stitch, referring to your machine's manual and the sidebar at right. Put topstitching thread in the looper and matching all-purpose thread in the needle. Practice the technique on a scrap of fabric before you begin.

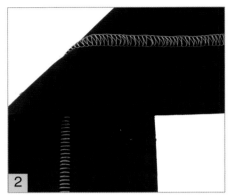

2-thread chain stitch

decorative chain stitching

Set your serger for chain stitch, referring to your machine's manual, and disengage the blade. The project instructions tell you which kind of thread you'll need. Cut a test fabric swatch plus several 2" (5 cm) squares of scrap fabric.

To test chain stitching, draw two or three lines on the wrong side of the test swatch, marking all the way across the surface. Place the swatch in the serger, aligning the needle with one of the lines. Sew all the way across the swatch. When you reach the end, put a scrap-fabric square in front of the presser foot and sew onto it, without cutting the threads.

Sew all the way across the scrap square. Then cut the chain-stitched threads between the test swatch and the scrap square. Swing the test swatch around in front of the presser foot and sew onto the next marked line without cutting the thread.

Turn the swatch right side up to see the decorative chain stitch. Adjust the thread tension to change the effect if you wish (page 18). Continue to experiment until you have the stitch you like.

3 Lay the belt back wrong side up on your work surface. With the fabric marker and 45-degree triangle as a guide, draw a diagonal line at one end of the piece. Then, working with the transparent ruler, draw additional diagonal lines spaced $1^1/2$" (4 cm) apart all along the surface of the belt back.

4 Draw another set of lines across the surface at the same interval but on the opposite diagonal, forming a grid.

5 Chain-stitch the belt back along each one of the marked lines.

6 With your sewing machine fitted with a needle appropriate for your fabric, sew $^1/2$" (1.3 cm) from all edges of the chain-stitched belt back. This line of stitching will secure the chain stitches and keep them from accidentally pulling out.

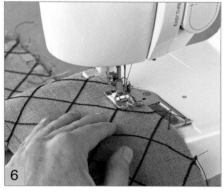

7 Press the stitched belt back and lay it flat. Center the lining on top and pin the layers together. With scissors or a rotary cutter, trim the back so it is the same size as the lining.

8 Fold one of the belt front pieces in half crosswise, right side out. Finger-press the fold. Working with the transparent grid ruler as a guide, draw a line from one end of the front to the fold, centering the line on the piece ($2^1/4$" [5.5 cm] from the long edges). Draw two more lines, each 1" (2.5 cm) from the edge, as shown in the photo. Do the same with the other front.

9 Put the beading foot on your serger and set the serger for 2-thread flatlock stitch, referring to your machine's manual. If they are not already in place, put topstitching thread in the looper and all-purpose thread in the needle. Practice the technique before stitching your project, following the instructions in the sidebar on the facing page.

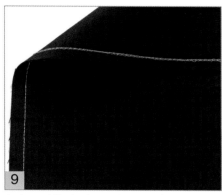

2-thread flatlock stitch

10 Unfold one of the marked belt fronts. Refold it on the center marked line. Place it in the serger with the cut end under the beading foot, referring to the sidebar on page 102. Lay one piece of cord in the foot and sew it on, stopping at the crease at the center of the fabric. To remove the piece from the serger, lift the presser foot and pull the fabric toward the back, pinching the stitches to keep them intact and working the handwheel back and forward as you pull. Pull the threads to the wrong side of the fabric, knot the ends, and trim.

hip belt

11 Working in the same way, sew another piece of cord to each of the other marked lines and to the lines on the other belt front.

12 Put the heavier needle in your sewing machine. Sew across the end of each belt front to secure the cords—stitch twice, once close to the cut edge and again about $1/4$" (6 mm) from the edge. Stitch slowly as you travel over the cord.

13 With the right sides together, pin and then sew the cord end of one front to one end of the chain-stitched back. Repeat to attach the other front at the other end of the back.

14 With the right sides together, sew the ends of the lining to the free ends of the fronts. Press open the seam allowances. At the front seams, finger-press the seam allowance, with the cord ends toward the chain-stitched back.

attaching cord with a beading foot

Set your serger for a 2-thread flatlock stitch. Put the beading foot on the serger. Your project directions tell you which threads to use. Cut a test swatch of your fabric.

To test the technique, draw a line all the way across the test swatch. Fold the fabric on the line. Place the fold under the beading foot, aligning it with the right edge of the cord guide, as shown in the top photo below. Lay the cord in the foot, extending it to the back edge of the fabric. Sew the cord to the folded edge.

Remove the swatch from the serger. Gently pull the fabric away from the cord so the stitches lie flat on the back and the cord sits smoothly on the face of the fabric, as shown in the bottom photo. If the cord doesn't lie flat, the stitches may be too tight—experiment to adjust the tension.

15 Lay the belt flat, still with wrong side out. Fold the fronts in half so the seams on the layers align and the lining faces the chain-stitched back. Arrange all the cord ends to extend from the center of one edge. Pin along both long edges, but don't pin near the cords.

16 Put the smaller needle back in your sewing machine. Sew one long edge of the belt from end to end. Sew the other long edge from each end toward the center, leaving a 6" (15 cm) opening at the center where the cords extend.

17 Turn the belt right side out. Press the edges, turning in the seam allowance along the opening. Hand-stitch the opening closed. Slide a bead onto the end of each cord, if you'd like.

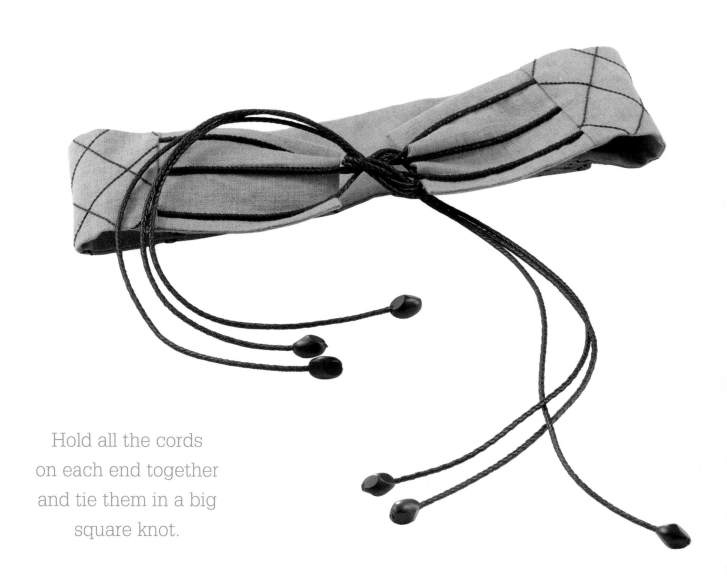

Hold all the cords on each end together and tie them in a big square knot.

tiered skirt

This peasant-style skirt has boho chic style and a flirty kick—thanks to the four tiers of gathered fabric that flow below the yoke. Each tier is gathered at the same time that it is stitched to the tier above it. No, it's not magic. It's the serger! Your standard sewing machine helps out with this project, too. There's a drawstring at the waist, so you're sure to get a perfect fit.

Size
- Small: hips 32" (81 cm)
- Medium: hips 35" (89 cm)
- Large: 40" (101.5 cm)

Machines and Feet
- 4- or 5-thread serger, with differential feed and rolled hem capability
- shirring foot
- rolled hem foot or plate (if needed for your serger)
- standard sewing machine

Materials
- 1/3 yd. (0.3 m) solid-color fabric, for yoke and drawstring
- 9 yd. (8.2 m) border-print fabric, for skirt tiers and yoke accent
- four spools of all-purpose sewing thread to match skirt fabric (five spools if you use a 4-thread overlock stitch)
- one spool of all-purpose sewing thread to match yoke accent fabric
- scrap of stabilizer (for buttonholes)

Notions and Tools
- tape measure
- ruler
- fabric marker
- scissors
- scrap paper and pencil
- pins
- bodkin or large safety pin (for inserting drawstring tie into casing)

Seam Allowance
1/2" (1.3 cm)

Note: See page 106 for the cutting list.

tiered skirt

Cutting List

Solid-color fabric

- Cut two yokes, each: Small: 7" deep x 17¹/2" wide (18 x 44.5 cm); Medium: 7" x 19¹/2" (18 x 49.5 cm); or Large: 7" x 22" (18 x 56 cm).

- Cut two drawstrings, each 1¹/2" x 30¹/2" (4 x 78 cm).

Border-print fabric

- Place width of all pieces on the lengthwise grain, parallel to the selvage.

- Cut tier 5 (to feature border): 8" deep x 275" wide (20.5 x 700 cm).

- Cut yoke accent (to feature border): Small: 3³/4" deep x 34" wide (9.5 x 87 cm); Medium: 3³/4" x 36" (9.5 x 92 cm); or Large: 3³/4" x 41" (9.5 x 104 cm).

- Cut tier 4: 7¹/2" deep x 165" wide (19 x 419 cm).

- Cut tier 3: 6" deep x 100" wide (15 x 254 cm).

- Cut tier 2: 6" deep x 60" wide (15 x 152 cm).

1 Measure, mark, and cut the pieces for the skirt, referring to the cutting list for your size. Pin an identifying label onto each piece.

2 Set the serger to a 3-thread overlock stitch, referring to your machine manual. Overlock all edges of both yoke pieces so they don't fray. Do not trim any of the fabric.

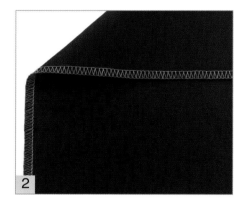

3-thread overlock stitch

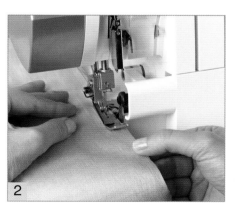

here's a hint!

If you mark the midpoint of the yoke with hand-basting, it will be easier to find it later.

3 To position the buttonholes for the drawstring, measure the long edge of one of the yoke pieces and mark the midpoint. Measure ³/4" (2 cm) to the right of the midpoint and mark a ⁵/8" (1.5 cm) vertical buttonhole 1¹/4" (3 cm) below the edge. Mark another buttonhole to the left of the midpoint the same way. (Check your machine manual for the correct way to mark a buttonhole.)

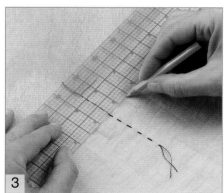

one-step gather-and-sew

With a shirring foot and your serger's differential feed, you can gather one piece of fabric while sewing it to a flat piece at the same time. This method is much faster than the traditional sewing-machine method of first stitching, and then gathering, the first piece before sewing it to the second.

Test the technique before you stitch your project. Put the shirring foot on your serger, set it to a 4-thread overlock stitch, and adjust the differential feed control to its highest setting so that it will gather the fabric (the lowest setting will stretch the fabric). Cut two test strips of fabric, one to be gathered and one to gather it onto. The strip to be gathered should be about three times as long as the other strip.

Place the longer strip in the serger, right side up. Place the shorter strip into the opening on the foot, right side down. Begin to sew. The long piece on the bottom will be gathered onto the shorter piece on top. Very cool!

Practice on scrap fabric until you are happy with the density of the gathers and are comfortable controlling the seam. The sidebar on page 52 explains how to adjust the tension settings to change the gathered effect.

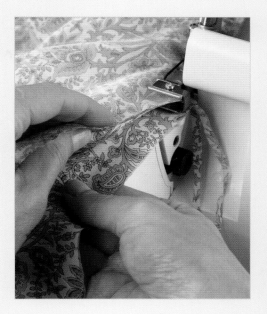

4 Place the scrap of stabilizer behind the marked buttonholes. Thread your sewing machine with thread to match the yoke fabric. Stitch the buttonholes and cut them open with a small scissors or seam ripper. Remove the excess stabilizer.

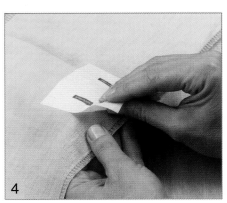

5 Set the sewing machine to a medium straight stitch. Place the yokes right sides together and sew along one 7" (18 cm) edge with 1/2" (1.3 cm) seam allowance. Next, sew the ends of the drawstring pieces together to make one long strip. Press open the seam allowances.

6 On one long edge (the top) of the yoke accent, fold and press 1/2" (1 cm) of fabric to the wrong side. Lay the yoke right side up. Lay the yoke accent right side up on top of it, aligning the bottom edge and the ends. Pin or baste the pieces together. Rethread the top of the sewing machine with thread to match the accent. Topstitch the top edge of the accent to the yoke.

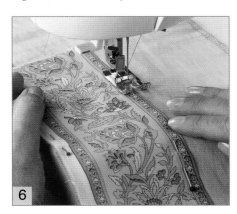

tiered skirt

7 Rethread the top of the machine with the thread to match the yoke fabric. With the right sides together, sew the 7" (18 cm) ends of the yoke together, forming a tube. Press open the seam allowance. On the top edge, fold and press 1 1/8" (2.5 cm) of fabric to the wrong side.

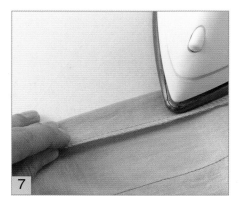

8 Stitch 7/8" (2.2 cm) from the fold, forming a casing.

9 Set your serger to a 4-thread overlock stitch (page 24). Attach the shirring foot and adjust the differential feed for gathering, referring to your machine manual and page 12. Test the technique before you begin, following the instructions in the sidebar on page 107.

10 Place the top edge of tier 3 right side up under the shirring foot. Place the bottom edge of tier 2 right side down in the shirring foot. Serge the pieces together. If tier 3 is not completely gathered onto tier 2, cut off the excess to make the ends even.

11 Repeat the process to gather and sew the top of tier 4 onto the bottom of tier 3, and then the top of tier 5 onto the bottom of tier 4.

12 Set your serger for a 3-thread rolled hem, referring to your manual and page 26. Practice the technique before stitching your project.

3-thread rolled hem

13 Finish the bottom edge of tier 5 with a 3-thread rolled hem.

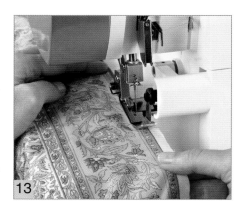

14 Fold the assembled skirt tiers vertically, aligning the raw edges and the ends of the gathered seams. Sew the raw edges together—with your sewing machine, or with your serger and the standard presser foot and 4-thread overlock stitch. If you sew them with the standard sewing machine, press open the seam allowances.

15 Attach the shirring foot and reset the serger for gathering. Gather the top edge of tier 2 (by itself).

16 Pin-mark the center front, center back, and side seams of yoke. Divide the skirt into four equal sections at the top edge of tier 2 and mark with pins. Right sides together, match pin markings of the skirt and yoke at center front, center back, and side seams. Adjust gathers to fit between the markings.

17 With your sewing machine set on a straight stitch, sew the yoke to the tiered skirt.

18 Reset your serger for a standard 3- or 4-thread overlock stitch. Sewing without fabric, stitch a chain of thread 65" (165 cm) long. Do not cut the thread chain.

here's a hint!

Before hemming tier 5, change the serger thread to match the color of the bottom of the border print.

19 Lay the drawstring right side up on your serger table and arrange the thread chain lengthwise on top. Fold the drawstring in half lengthwise, around the thread chain. Starting at the end of the chain that is still attached to the serger, serge the long edges of the drawstring together. Be careful not to catch the enclosed chain in the stitches.

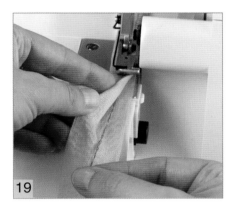

20 As shown in the photos, gently pull the free end of the thread chain to turn the drawstring right side out.

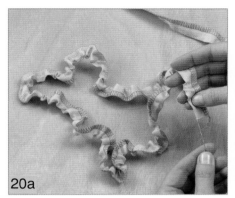
20a

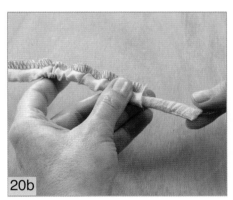
20b

21 Press the drawstring. With the bodkin, thread the drawstring through the casing at the top of the yoke. (You can also feed the drawstring through by attaching a safety pin to one end.) Tie an overhand knot at each end of the drawstring so that it can't slip into the casing.

Slip into your skirt, snug the drawstring to fit, and dance the night away.

Creative Publishing international

Copyright © 2008
Creative Publishing international, Inc.

First published in the United States of America by
Creative Publishing international, Inc., a member of
Quayside Publishing Group
400 First Avenue North, Suite 300
Minneapolis, MN 55401
1-800-328-3895
www.creativepub.com

ISBN-13: 978-1-58923-350-8
ISBN-10: 1-58923-350-6

10 9 8 7 6 5 4 3 2 1

Library of Congress Cataloging-in-Publication Data

Hanson, Becky, 1955-
  Quick and easy sewing with your serger : 15 easy-
sew projects that build skills too / Becky Hanson.
       p. cm. -- (Easy singer style)
  Includes index.
  ISBN 1-58923-350-6
  1. Serging. 2. Machine sewing. I. Title. II. Series.

  TT713.H34 2008
  646.2'044--dc22   2 007049071
                                         CIP

Technical Editor: Carol Spier
Copy Editor: Kristy Mulkern
Proofreader: Catherine Broberg
Page Layout: Leslie Haimes

Printed in China

acknowledgments

Special thanks to Marleen Baker, Jeanine Jones, and Nicole Smith for
their contributions.

about the author

Becky Hanson received her first sewing machine at age nine and has
been sewing ever since. She is the education manager for SINGER
Sewing Company and also serves as the education manager for SVP
Worlwide Inc. She is the creator and host of a new series of instructional
DVDs for SINGER sewing machines and sergers. At home, Becky creates
couture millinery, a craft she studied in London, England.

about the contributors

Marleen Baker holds a B.S. in Clothing and Textiles from Eastern
Michigan University and is an education consultant for SINGER Sewing
Company. She also worked with a major fabric retailer as a district home
economist, designing projects and teaching. A mother of two adult
daughters, she lives in Wisconsin with her husband, Jerry.

Jeanine Jones teaches embroidery, quilting, serging, and home décor
sewing. She also runs her own home decorating business. She has created projects for sewing schools, web sites, and magazines, and is an education consultant for SINGER Sewing Company. Her articles have
appeared in *Creative Machine Embroidery*, *Quilting & Embroidery*, and
Designs in Machine Embroidery.

Nicole Smith is the coauthor of *Fashion DIY: 30 Ways to Craft Your Own
Style* (Sixth & Spring, 2007). She was formerly a sewing editor for
Cutting Edge magazine and has also worked for *Teen People* and
Seventeen. She cofounded Appliance Clothing in 2005 and teaches class-
es at Make Workshop in New York City.

suppliers

Sergers, Sewing Machines, and Accessories
SINGER Sewing Company
1224 Heil Quaker Boulevard
LaVergne, TN 37086
615-213-0880
www.singerco.com
www.sewingideas.com
www.singerbookstore.com
SINGER sewing machines and sergers are available at authorized SINGER retailers.

Fabric
Benartex Inc.
1359 Broadway, Suite 1100
New York, NY 10018
212-840-3250
www.benartex.com

Fabric Traditions
519 8th Avenue, 19th Floor
New York, NY 10018
212-279-5710
www.fabrictraditions.com

Hancock Fabrics Inc.
One Fashion Way
Baldwyn, MS 38824
877-322-7427
www.hancockfabrics.com

Jo-Ann Fabric and Craft Stores
5555 Darrow Rd.
Hudson, OH 44236
888-739-4120
www.joann.com

Mood Fabrics
225 W. 37th Street, 3rd Floor
New York, NY 10018
212-730-5003
www.moodfabrics.com

Textile Fabrics
2717 Franklin Road
Nashville, TN 37204
615-297-5346
www.textilefabricstore.com

Beads, Buttons, and Embellishments
Ghee's
2620 Centenary Boulevard #2-250
Shreveport, LA 71104
318-226-1701
www.ghees.com

JHB International, Inc.
1955 South Quince Street
Denver, CO 80231
303-751-8100
www.buttons.com

M & J Trimming
1008 Sixth Avenue
New York, NY 10018
800-965-8746
www.mjtrim.com

also available

Easy SINGER Style
Quick and Easy Window Treatments
ISBN: 978-1-58923-351-5

Easy SINGER Style
Pattern-free Fashion & Accessories
ISBN: 978-1-58923-312-6

Easy SINGER Style
Pattern-free Home Accents
ISBN: 978-158923-320-1

SINGER Simple Sewing Guide
ISBN: 978-1-58923-313-3

SINGER Simple Home Décor Handbook
ISBN: 978-1-58923-314-0

SINGER Simple Mending and Repair
ISBN: 978-1-58923-340-9

SINGER Simple Decorative
Machine Stitching
ISBN: 978-1-58923-341-6

index

a

accessories, for sewing, 13–15. *See also* fashion and accessories projects

b

beading foot, 12–13
  hip belt project, 98–103
belt project, 98–103
binding, in blanket project, 58–61
blades, 8, 10–11, 20
blanket with overlock binding project, 58–61
blind-hem foot, 13
  simple curtain project, 74–77
bow, in wire-edged ribbon project, 66–69
brush, 15

c

chain stitches, 10, 21, 25
  hip belt project, 98–103
clothing, projects to remake, 35–55
cone adapter, 14
cording foot, 12
corners, sewing of, 20–21
cover stitches, 21, 25–26
  pillow project, 62–65
  tunic transformation project, 36–39
cozy blanket with overlock binding project, 58–61
curtain projects
  simple curtains, 74–77
  tiebacks, 78–81
curves, sewing of, 20–21
cutting tools, 32–33

d

differential feed, 11–12

e

embellished skirt project, 40–43

f

fabric grain, 31
fashion and accessories projects, 82–109
faux vintage sweater project, 50–55
feed dogs, 11–12
flatlock stitches, 21, 26
fringed wrap project, 88–93
fringed wrap project, 88–93

g

gathering
faux vintage sweater project, 50–55
  tiered skirt project, 104–109
gimp foot, 13
grain, of fabrics, 31

h

hand-sewing needles, 15
hip belt project, 98–103
home décor projects, 56–81

k

knife blade. *See* blades

l

large-eye hand-sewing needle, 15
liquid seam sealant, 15
loopers, 8, 10, 14, 20, 39

m

marking tools, 32
measurements, 31, 33

n

needles, 9, 15, 19

o

overedge stitches, 26, 27
  embellished skirt project, 40–43
overlock stitches, 21, 24
  blanket project, 58–61

p

pillow project, 62–65
pins/pin cushions, 33
piping, in tieback project, 78–81
presser feet, 8, 12–13, 18, 19

reversible cover-stitch pillow project, 62–65
ribbing, in t-shirt project, 44–49
ribbons
  ribbon-trimmed table runner project, 70–73
  wire-edged ribbon bow project, 66–69
rolled hem stitch, 26–27
rosettes project, 94–97
rosettes project, 94–97

s

safety stitch, 24, 25
scissors, 32
seam rippers, 33
seams, 19–20
sergers, 5, 7
  accessories for, 13–15
  basics of sewing with, 17–21
  how they stitch, 8
  parts of, 9–13
  types of, 9
shirring foot, 12
skirt projects
  embellished skirt, 40–43
tiered skirt, 104–109
spool caps, 14
stitches
  size of, 18–20
  types of, 23–27
stitch finger, 11
sweater project, 50–55

t

table runner project, 70–73
taping foot, 13
tassels, in thread-chain project, 84–87
tension, setting of, 10, 18, 19
thread-chain tassel project, 84–87
threading tips, 14, 18
threads, 29–31
tieback project, 78–81
tiered skirt project, 104–109
t-shirt shrug project, 44–49
tunic transformation project, 36–39
tweezers, 13–14

w

wire-edged ribbon bow project, 66–69
wrap project, 88–93

y

yarn application foot, 13